MY WOMB

Sadaff Habib
My Womb

Cover Design and Illustration by: Rein G. Layout Design by: Rein.G
www.fiverr.com/reindrawthings

Published by BooxAI
ISBN: 978-965-578-904-1

MY WOMB

A COLLECTION OF 108 POEMS OF UNEARTHING,
UNRAVELING AND RE-BIRTHING

SADAFF HABIB

CONTENTS

To the one who created me,
To the other who liberated me,
To the two who birthed me,
To the third who pushed me,
To all those who came before me,
And to all those who will come after me.

INTRODUCTION

An End to a Beginning, a Beginning to an End

Wounds. Pain. Hurt. Tears. We run from them a mile away. The slightest discomfort that arises we wish to change immediately. In my journey so far, I have realized that in our deepest and darkest of wounds, the ones we don't like to think of, let alone feel or be reminded of in any way. Those wounds are as precious as gold. They are our gold. In those depths of sadness, betrayal, and loss lie our gifts waiting each moment to be born.

Ultimately, all those tears are pearls of wisdom and all those lonely moments of heartache, a balm to the soul. This is not a realization that we have or that can come easily to us when we are shrouded and entangled in sadness. It certainly did not come to me immediately. But it came to me as I journeyed on, and I realized that it is possible. It is possible to be in a storm of life and yet watch detached. It is possible, and I believe it is part of our purpose on this earth. For a long time, I questioned, "Why am I here?" What my purpose is. The answer that

I grow and learn to understand each day, is simple. I am here to be the best version of myself. Not of you, or my family, nor to meet anyone's expectations of what I should or should not be, not to pigeon- hole into a role, not to satisfy a criteria, but to simply be me. Because when I return to the Creator, and I am asked how I lived, I want to proudly say I lived as no one and nothing but me. All of me in a moment. But to arrive at me, a lot of shredding was and continues to be involved. Letting go of conditioning, shreds of expectation and denial, can take time and I have grown to accept that this is okay. To return to my original mind, my original state, to return to that blissful moment; for that moment, all the pain is worth it.

And it is not always about pain. Sometimes, the sight of a baby green parrot pecking for food in an area otherwise frequented by crows can be a sight of grace. Other times, a little Sofia showing you her doll can bring back your lost smile. Yet other times, the silent ever watching blue sky can share its wisdom.

It is always there. Never far but very near. Our salvation, our thirst, our want for happiness, is but a breath away, provided our hearts are wide open to receive. To open our hearts to such grace, that is our noble mission. To achieve it, we must purify. To purify, we must walk through those shadows that we hurriedly lock away.

You may wonder why I call this poetry collection My Womb. Biology dictates that a woman has a womb to procreate, to birth another human. In mythology our wombs hold much more power, grace and healing. The womb symbolizes the sacred feminine, creation and life. It symbolizes regeneration and nurturing not only for others but for herself. A woman's precious womb can heal her wounds and re-birth her into all that she is.

Why 108 poems? If you add 1+0+8 you arrive at 9 and it takes 9 months for a baby to grow in the Womb before it is ready to greet the world. 108 is a spiritual number of great significance. There are 108 beads in a Hindu mala (rosary). There are 108 sacred sites all over India. There are 108 stars in Chinese astrology and 108 marma points in Ayurveda. The diameter of the Sun is approximately 108 times the diameter of the Earth, and the average distance from the Earth to the Sun is about 108 times the Sun's diameter. Similarly, the distance from the Earth to the Moon is approximately 108 times the Moon's diameter. Isn't that so special?

This poetry collection unfolds as the journey of a heroine through 108 poems. Her odyssey commences in the depths of childhood scars and unwept tears, only to emerge on the other side—from a wounded little girl who lost her voice to a woman proclaiming her divine feminine essence. She questions spirituality, dances with nature, and embraces the full spectrum of her being—capturing the essence of all that she is and continues to become.

I invite you on this journey through shadows, through moments of light, through more shadows, through self-doubt, through the divine feminine, and conversations with grace. Let these poems serve as your own compassionate healing hand.

My prayer for you is that through these words you

find your healing grace.

With eternal light, love and blessings,
Sadaff

The Fire

Let the heat of your flames burn me to the ground, let the warmth of your embers penetrate my wounds. Oh, holy fire, accept my agony as a sacrifice to you.

Don't Yell

Don't yell; it hurts.

It hurts my ears, it hurts my heart,

it hurts my existence.

Existence, 4-year-old me does not know the word,

but I feel it.

I feel that I am.

I know that something thumps inside of me,

threatening to burst each time you yell.

Each time you fight, each time you hit Mummy.

Please, I beg you don't yell.

Is it my fault?

Are you unhappy because I am here?

Are you unhappy that I was born?

Don't yell, Papa. Don't yell.

My heart beats faster than I have learnt to count.

I tremble with fear, I shrivel with cold.

I don't know where to hide.

Are you not supposed to protect me?

I see Mama cry.

Don't yell, Papa. I beg you.

But you do not hear my cry.

You do not see my pain.

You do not hold me.

You do not love me.

You have left me.

A Child Soldier Is Born

I felt your pain.

He kicked you, and my stomach ached

He pushed you, and I got knocked.

He dragged you by your hair,

and I felt my head go numb.

You collapsed in pain and I died inside,

seeing you motionless.

Mama.

I felt each slap, each push, each punch.

Helpless, I watched,

Too young to defend you,

Too scared of Papa.

He was too big for me,

Not knowing what to do.

I cried.

I prayed.

I cried.

I prayed.

Tears unwiped;

Prayers unheard.

Frozen in fear, I watched you cry for help.

I ran to the kitchen to find a knife,

Its sharpness I knew from the vegetables you chopped.

The cold steel would protect me, you, us, from whom?

It was my job to protect you.

It was my job to shield sister.

It was my job to take care of us all.

The murder of innocence,

The funeral of my 7-year-old self—

All with the shine of a blade

As I walked toward you, knife in hand.

Papa took it away from me and violently shook you.

Terrified.

Not until later in life did I understand

I died in that moment.

From your child, I became your soldier.

School Bags

School bags,

A memory floats from the past.

A friend's school bag I once admired flashes past.

Because at 10 years, she was prettier than me,

smarter than me.

And if I had the same school bag,

I too would be pretty and smart.

Maybe my parents would then love me,

see me, hear me.

A complex ingrained,

A life in vain,

A schoolbag carried for years.

Until my shoulders were too weary,

Begged me to let go.

Broken backed, I gathered courage

To allow myself to believe

School bag or not,

Pretty or not,

Smart or not,

Loved or not,

Seen or not,

Heard or not,

I was always enough.

Happy Birthday, Son

Excited, eager, it is my 13th birthday.

Officially a teenager, a rite of passage, a crossover.

Cake for me and lots of presents

And love from Mummy and Papa and Sister.

I am sure Papa will bring me a gift tonight.

It is my birthday after all.

I am ready, dressed up and happy.

And Papa is here!

Empty, with no gift.

Empty, with no excitement.

Empty, with no happiness.

It is my birthday; my heart cries.

Never mind, I tell myself.

We will cut cake and be a happy family.

I mean, play a happy family.

Request me a song papa on the radio.

A fight. An argument.

Should Mummy call the radio or Papa?

I should have never asked for anything.

I should have never asked to be seen or to be heard.

I should have never been born.

Harsh words. Sad words. Tears run down my cheeks

My birthday is over.

Papa requests a song.

Happy birthday, Sadaff, may he have many more.

And I am a boy.

He does not correct them.

He gets angry at Mummy.

Embarrassed by his failure—the adult in me reasons.

13-year-old me cries in anger.

Body changes, puberty, no friends,

Fat, ugly, geeky,

Unloved,

And now I am a boy

No one ever sees my pain.

Wanting to Die

I wanted to die.

I wanted someone, anyone to rescue me, to save me,

to help me,

help me, save me from myself, save me from the anger,

the shouting, the cruelty of the world, the unsteadiness

of my world inside and outside,

to show me that there is a better world—another world

out there

where I am loved

and cared for,

where I am felt for,

where my tears are seen,

where I am beautiful.

You see, at the age of 14, I decided I was worthless.

I decided that I was an ugly duckling.

I decided that I would never be loved.

I decided death would serve me.

Not knowing what death really meant,

I decided it was a mistake to be born.

Your Marriage Took It All

Your marriage saw no room for me,

For my tears, for my growth, for my fears,

My dreams, my hopes.

Your marriage took it all,

Snatched me up in its embers of ego and pride,

Chewed me and spat me out in bones.

Between wiping your tears and listening to your anger,

Mine fell unheard, unseen, unwiped.

When my feelings became too much for my gentle heart,

I silenced them into the darkest tunnels,

into the deepest folds of my being.

I told myself I had to be strong, to take care of you,

That tears and the sharp pain in my heart from

the dagger of your words must be quieted,

Must be killed

So that I can be strong for you.

There was no room for me to share my pain.

The growing pains of a teenager,

The insults from a teacher,

The snares from fellow little creatures—

There was no room for my aches, my words, my pains.

It was all about you and him.

Never about me.

Never do I recall a day I was asked how am I?

Am I happy in school?

Am I treated well?

And so I found my peace in books,

In words I found friendship;

In pages I found love.

Maybe this is why I do not wish to have a child

Because the child in me died an untimely death.

So quick, so swift, no time for a funeral.

And before I knew it, I turned into a woman,

Nursing the little girl, I once was,

Walking through the same shadows, to heal herself,

Never understood, never accepted.

All the pain pumps in the veins of my heart,

And now they throb for my attention.

Regretful, I allowed this to happen.

Grateful, I can salvage the situation.

A path of healing set before me

Decorated with buried tears and unleashed anger

I know not who I am other than your savior

Who am I outside these embers of violence

I call home?

Who am I meant to be other than your protector?

What am I outside this 'family'?

Nobody Loved Me

Nobody loved me.

Papa did not see my tears and did not love me.

For if he loved me, he would never hit you.

For if he loved me, he would see that each blow

to your face was a blow to my tender heart.

For if he loved me, he would have knelt down and

wiped my tears and hugged me tight and promised me

that he would never hit you again.

And we would have lived happily ever after.

But there was no happily ever after.

From violence to poison words,

My broken heart grieved for a father and grief turned

into anger and hate.

Year on year, I housed two venomous guests

in my tender heart, anger and hate.

This was not me;

This was not my nature.

Oh, it pained my heart.

Hate pounded and threatened to smother me.

What could I do?

He was my dad.

There was only so much I could cry and shout.

And I hated him,

How I hated him.

Many moons passed and the pain grew

into a tree of its own.

Lost was the little girl tender and hopeful of the world

trusting in its goodness.

No longer safe did she feel for everywhere

she saw monsters.

Packing bags, unpacking bags, a broken home,

a band-aid home

Until the day I broke

And ripped down the walls built around

my tender heart, to protect it from hurt or cry.

Prayer and tears once again became an ally

As brick by brick, the wall came down

And my heart came back to life

And breath by breath I welcomed joy.

A Psychic Garbage Can—No More

You used me as your psychic garbage can.

Each time there was a fight,

You never, not once, thought I am just a child.

Was that fair? I ask.

Was that just? I shout.

And all my shouts and screams were unheard

Because as a child, I only wanted your love.

And so I listened.

You said bad things about Papa and I listened

Your words ignited embers of hate in my heart

as I listened.

If I hated him, you would love me.

I still had your love

And that was all that mattered to me, Mummy.

You were my world.

I was but a child, Mummy.

Why?

Why?

And today when I cry,

When I wish to heal and the little girl

in me demands answers,

You run and hide behind your pain,

Behind your victimhood

You blame me.

Why?

Why is it so difficult to simply say sorry

So that I finally know that you loved me

and did not only use me?

Why does it still hurt so much?

When I thought I had healed from all this,

I have to save myself.

There is no one coming to save me.

I must save myself.

I will save myself.

I will protect myself so that I am never used again.

I swear to love myself so much that no person's words

ever stab me

I know I will get no answers from you;

No hugs will ever be forthcoming.

And so I see I am alone,

Yet again alone.

Alone as a child, alone as an adult,

Whose life did I live until now?

Whose life am I living now?

Your expectations, your dreams, your desires

Papa's hopes, Papa's dreams

Who am I?

Why am I here?

What did I want?

What do I want from this life?

This life is mine and only mine.

It is not yours.

It was never yours to own.

Yes, you birthed me.

But I am a child of God

And I have my own life

Not yours, not Papa's.

This is my life,

And I chose to live it my way

And only my way,

And I promise myself today.

For as long as I live,

I will ask myself each day,

What will make me happy today?

For I am my mother, my father,

my brother and my sister

There is no one for me but me,

And I will cherish myself

And blossom to my higher soul's calling.

This is my life,

A gift from God to love to treasure to hope

without measure

And I make this promise today.

I choose to live my way each day.

The Ultimate Tragedy

The tragedy was never that you thought me unworthy

That you thought me unlikely

That you dismissed my voice

That you discredited my views

Or criticized my talents.

The tragedy was always

That I believed you

That I allowed you to step on me

That I welcomed you to drown my voice

That I bowed to your opinions of me,

of my life, of my choices.

The tragedy was I accepted it.

Healing
From Ashes

Let me rest in these ashes,
oh pray let me rest, let me be,
please let me be,
for once let me heal.

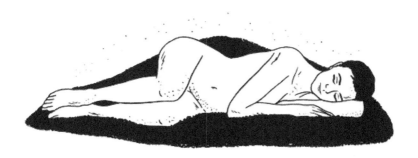

Is Death So Bad?

Unloved, unheard, unseen

A life not so long past

Where my own threw me to the enemy

An arrow shot through my heart

A betrayal carried on

For rebirth is real

Never understood, always mistaken

An anguish to save the world

A responsibility not mine and yet taken

Shoulders hunched from the weight

A light I no longer see

Abandoned by God

Left to die alone

And so why is death so bad?

The Abyss

A void as deep and dark as the depths of the sea

A darkness never ending

A ghostly pitch black

A love lost

A love I seek

To save me

I still do not know whose life I am living.

Am I living?

Or am I dead?

Or am I an empty vessel that shuffles?

I am still uncovering who I am.

It is dead;

It is all dead.

And I am alive.

And yet I feel buried in the depths of the sand

In an abyss of memories I am falling,

A darkness welcoming,

A homecoming

Of tears and fears.

And here I am—

Bare and broken,

Ready for another war.

The lesson I am here to learn

For my soul

Is to love me,

To love my shadow.

I cannot believe that was my life;

I cannot believe this is my life.

Maybe neither is real.

A deep pain lodged in my heart

Threatens to break;

It needs to dissolve

Permanently

Forever and ever

Never to return again

Because despite myself my heart beats,

And as long as I live I continue to explore

this world and its creatures,

I surrender.

I give up.

I give up pretending and trying.

I give it all up.

I give up breathing.

I give up living.

To heal, I must journey to the deepest darkness

inside of me

So that I can light my own candle inside.

There is no other way to live.

Either I light a candle

Or let the darkness engulf me.

Swallow me whole.

Let it wrap its arms around me.

Maybe it will be warm.

Who knows?

Maybe the darkness is not so bad after all.

Maybe it will soothe the hurts of many a decade.

I choose to be nothing and no one but me.

I choose to only be me.

But who is me?

There is a deep abyss of pain buried inside.

I must let it out.

I must heal

Inside out.

Do Not Mistake That I See Myself as Weak

Do not mistake that I see myself as weak,

For I know in the depths of my pain lies my strength.

But what am I to do from here?

Where am I to go?

Is there a place, a heart that will understand

and accept me

As I am

No edits?

Is there someone who can be there for me?

Who can hold me in my darkest hour and deepest pain

and console me of a brighter day?

Is this a prayer too steep to make?

Or is it my soul's lesson to seek solace from none

but itself?

I did my best as a child,

Knowing not the impact of drowning my sorrow,

My insides too soft for this world

And yet as a woman, people only see my strength,

My vulnerability in mask and what an act I put on.

The Oscar of Life is surely mine for the taking.

As I wipe away tears of another time

And carry on to the next scene.

Another act, another day—

How far can I continue

When my soul is threatening to break all my well-

constructed dams?

Where will I end up on this path of life?

The world, my atlas,

And my heart, a map of my fate.

A Human in Pain

How do I love when I am not loved?

Care when I am not cared for?

Smile when it means nothing?

Laugh when it is but empty sound?

When and how the family thread snapped

Years of bondage released

Time took its toll.

Words made foul relations of years

Pain, tears,

An enigma of fears.

Healing needed

Patience and love, my tender heart pleaded.

No one heeded.

In anguish, I cried.

I cannot show up for you until I forgive;

I cannot be the person you want me to be

Because that person is a lie.

All your thoughts and views imposed on me are a lie.

They are not me.

I am not them.

Only now am I discovering who I am,

Nurturing the candle of truth that was always lit,

A tender flame with the might of a volcano.

I am not you; I never was.

I am neither your crutch nor your crane;

I am a human in pain.

A love not forthcoming from you

So give me time, I beg.

To be, to understand, to live—

To for once, just be

To simply be me.

Would It Be So Bad to Slow Down?

Why did I have so much going on?

Why as a society do we revere those who claim

they have no time?

The acclaimed multi-taskers, the busy,

the rushing ones,

Running to what I wonder.

Death?

Pause does not exist

Because it is believed it does not pay.

Was I one of them?

Do I now look down on them?

Am I now better than them?

Have I found the answer that they all seek?

No.

For if I think I am better, I return to the shackles

that I claim to have broken.

For if I look down on them, sooner or later I will fall.

For if I have found the answer,

I would no longer be a seeker.

No.

I know nothing.

And yet I am everything.

If we all stopped to breathe, would the world end?

If we said "no" more times than "yes,"

would we be found out?

If we paused, looking to each other with respect

and listening to our hearts, what would we lose?

If we all know that each heartbeat is a promise

and each breath not a guarantee of the next,

Then why do we ceaselessly and mindlessly continue?

And in our wake leave many a soul abandoned

and dishonored?

If we could all spend a moment to hold each other,

would it be so bad

To give a hug and let it last a moment longer?

Would the stock market crash if we all slowed down?

And even if it did, what of it?

Would we not get up and pull each other up

and climb back up?

Time immemorial, there have been losses and gains.

So would it be so bad to pause?

Would it be so bad to slow down?

A Contract to Live My Truth

Family ties

Unspoken binds

Expectations, voices, wants

Ambitions squished

Thoughts channeled.

Who am I outside their thoughts, their ideas?

I do not want any of that.

Even if I do not belong, and, the black sheep,

Is it so bad?

Do not I only belong to myself?

Why do they limit and narrow?

And why do they fear

And impose on me?

Why do I accept this fear?

It is not mine.

Their thoughts are not mine;

Their opinions are not mine;

Their beliefs are not mine.

I wish to return to my original state.

The unwritten blank slate

Break away all connections

To their ideologies and philosophies.

I reject them all.

I no longer accept any of it

I do not accept their views

On how I choose to breathe.

I choose to live my life the way that I wish.

I choose to live my way—

Only my way.

I no longer care for their thoughts about me.

They were never my concern.

I decide what is right and wrong for me.

I choose my people, my tribe for me.

I do not control,

And I do not allow to be controlled.

I break all unwritten contracts,

Vows never consciously consented.

I hold to one promise

To live only my truth.

Will You?

If I lay my scars for you to see,

Will you judge me?

Or will you pick me up to heal?

If I show you my deepest wounds

Those that have travelled with me

like faithful companions

Through many a soul journey,

Will you mock me?

Or will you hold my hand and caress me?

If I share my darkest desires

A part that scares me most,

Will you run and hide?

If I lie naked in all my truth,

Will you clothe me?

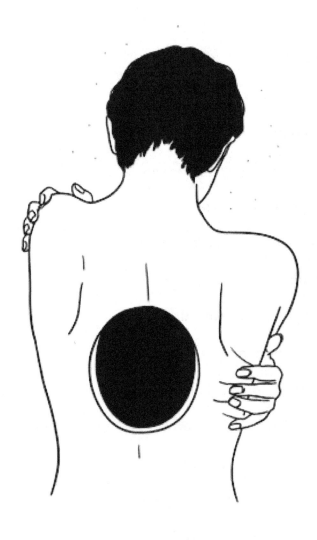

I Am Enough

I have gorged self-help books, since 16.

Are they another escape?

An escape from the reality of myself

The question keeps arising—am I enough?

A stellar student, an acing career,

yet when I least expect I question "am I good enough?"

When I am busy making excuses, in quiet moments,

in meditation I see the glare, "are you enough?".

I realize that as much as I thought the limiting belief

had ended,

Here it is in its full glory,

Demanding and commanding my attention.

What if I decide this time to starve it,

Starve it into death, into oblivion, into non-existence,

Starve it from its nutrient of negativity,

vitamin of attention?

What if this time, I look at it in the face and say,

Ah, here you are again; well, I have news for you.

I am enough.

I have always been enough.

The fact that I have blood soaring my veins,

the fact that I breathe, the fact that my heart beats,

the fact that I exist to hear your insolent cries

The fact that I face up to your cries and shout no more.

I am enough; I have more news for you.

I was enough from my first breath and I will remain

enough until my last breath.

Nothing and no one can deny my existence.

For as I exist, I am enough.

For as life throbs through my veins, I am enough.

So pester me no more, for your efforts are in vain.

I challenge you to this dual, so dare if you must.

For I know I shall triumph,

For I am enough.

Melting, Shedding, Burning

Everything is melting away.

I am melting away.

The walls built inside

The half felt emotions

The deep buried pains

Scars that never healed

Slowly and painfully melt away,

Like hot wax on a candle.

Without the burn, there is no wax.

And so these tears soothe the pain

Dissolve all these hurts and cracks

All those half-baked promises

All the brokenness and incompleteness

To melt it all away,

To wash it away in the sea.

Surrender it to the breasts of Mother Ocean.

Give room to my burdens in your pregnant waves;

I pray.

Dissolve them as they kiss the sand,

For I am not sure I can do this on my own.

Guide me to the end, Mother Nature.

I wish to see this through,

For I know on the other side of this heartache and tears

Is tranquility

Of a different kind,

A lasting kind

One that I have not felt before,

One that is real.

A true reflection of me,

For as these layers painfully peel away,

I wonder if the snake shedding its skin feels

so much pain,

But what's more painful is rotting

In the same patterns of behavior,

taking the same turns.

It is time to say goodbye to all that is learnt.

A pyre of emotions to burn

And so I let these tears flow

And vow to honor it all to the end,

For I have made a promise to salute each feeling

of mine

To give space to every emotion

Space denied by the world

And now I hold space for me and I pray

for my salvation

To allow myself to one day

Hold space for the rest of creation.

The Basket of Dead

I die every day

And yet I die not.

I live every day

Yet I live not.

What is this paradox of life and death

that you speak of, I cry.

I am alive; I know who I am.

No, you do not.

No one does.

You walk around carrying the ghosts of your past.

They are dead.

The little girl of 7

Dead.

The teenager of 14 dead.

The adult of 21 dead.

So why do you carry a basket full of the dead?

Even the woman you thought you were yesterday

is dead.

The woman you think you are today will die today,

And tomorrow you will be born again.

With each sunset, the cycle repeats

And yet you hold on.

Hold on to what? I say.

Is there really anything to hold on to?

If all the past is but a ghost, why does it hurt me so?

Why does the body carve a roadmap of my pain?

I do not wish to relive anything or carry any ghosts,

But yet to get to where I want,

I must walk through those shadows.

I now see why I need to walk through

the shadows first—

To bid them adieu because I carry them.

As I finally say goodbye,

My burden lessens

And I lighten.

It is time to drop all the dead—

To bury the ghosts of the past for good.

All my past selves are gone.

Today's self will be gone tomorrow,

For truly nothing

belongs to me

Not even me.

Oh, Healing Grace

Oh, healing grace,

Where do I find you?

I know not except that you exist.

Guide me to eternity,

The place of infinity,

A blossoming an unfolding,

An uncurling and unfurling,

Like a sunflower kissed by the sun.

A place of peace,

Of love

Where my body is vibrant

Where my breath is strong

And mind vigor

And I have the strength to carry on.

Oh healing grace,

Show me some light

A simple ray would do

I ask not for much

Just enough to get me through.

The Healing Horse

I thought rage was wrong.

I thought the anger that I felt thumping in my throat,

threatening an eruption was wrong.

Something not to be felt

Something unladylike, Even ungrateful

And punishable by God.

But then I got on a healing horse,

And it galloped to places I had long shut away

Knowingly and unknowingly,

And it would drop me in front of doors

of memories past,

Encouraging and demanding that I walk through.

"This is the only way" my horse would say

And so I would

Open the door of sometimes a quiet cry and

sometimes a tornado of anger.

And it would pour

And solitude I would seek

And even after being on this journey for so long,

From time to time the healing horse comes along,

nudging me to open yet another door—

A door I thought I had walked through

But perhaps not with an open heart.

And there I go again surfing a sea of emotions

left unaddressed

Until nothing remains to be said.

And sometimes

Even now

The anger rocks from within.

And it creeps up and the people you thought you

had forgiven are not

And the words that scarred you sound again

And you curse yourself for believing them.

And so it is

Forgiveness to me is what is banging on the door,

Love to me is what I need to pour

On these ancient wounds.

How much longer? I ponder.

"Forever more", my trusted horse says.

The Creator Within

I carve a life for myself

Out of love, energy and divine union,

Looking in to look out,

Asking soul before mind or body,

Ignoring thought,

Tuning in to heart and soul,

Praying for divine guidance to light the way,

To show the path of this new way of life

A way of life not lived before

A life where the inside matters more than the outside

Where the inside reflects the outside

Where blessings arise because of inner goodwill

Where love is poured from above

And mystic energy no longer a dream

But a homecoming.

A realization into the depths of my soul

An understanding of *Maya*[1]

A new way to live

Where outside pressure no longer penetrates

Where desires no longer dictate

And each moment is greeted with equanimity

Bowed down in serenity

The path is bright and bold

Lit in ecstasy and gold.

A new world awaits

As creator and creation.

---

[1] *Maya* a philosophy in the ancient Vedas connoted to be a veil that covers our real nature and the real nature of the world around us.

A Combined Consciousness

A pride of you in me and of me in me

You inside of me and I inside of you.

This is what I felt when I saw you, Papa.

Holding hands and staring into each other's eyes

for eternity,

It was like looking into myself through you

Our consciousness, a combined love

Inside one another we are.

So was it really you that I saw

Or your consciousness in me?

Me, My Own Foe

I finally thought I had it all figured out:

Who I was and what I was about,

Only to find it was only a scratch, a dent I had made

Into the great mystery.

I thought I had now mastered the art of self-love,

Only to find I still had to learn to nurture this love,

Learn to befriend the little me

To allow the big me to grow.

With an ache in my heart,

A sorrow difficult to explain,

I realized I have always been my own enemy.

The emails I never sent,

The calls I never made,

The people I never approached

Because I stopped me.

I doubted me

And as much as my roots played their part

And society ran its course,

The truth remained.

All along my shadow became my enemy,

Incessant doubt, criticism, words I told myself

That I would not dare tell a child.

I thought I had surpassed it all

Outgrown all these limitations

And yet from time to time,

I find them creep about.

Those times I seek validation outside

From loved ones mostly,

And when my hunger is not fed,

A sense of loss sweeps over.

The only compliment I will ever need

Is from me.

And this I thought I knew,

Only to find I had not seen the lesson through

Until I understand I am enough

And no perfection is needed

Nor is competition with others warranted.

I will continue to be my own foe.

Healing To Sparkle

No one tells you healing can be messy.

There are incessant tears to release,

Boxes of tissue to get through,

Endless snot to blow through,

Pain in your depths to let go of,

Knots of rage, anger, years of sadness to untangle

And yet after all is said and done,

A calmness settles

A stillness of profound wisdom

A peace unique.

Unspoken, unread, unwritten

And in that resting wisdom,

Your heart smiles.

Alive to the rainbows in its sinews

Alive to a myriad of possibilities.

In that wisdom, you emerge

Anew, and yet not, for it is still you.

But nothing remains the same,

For you are wisened,

For your wound, though healed,

the scar a telling truth remains.

A tattoo of your voyage of pain and triumph

As you straighten and wipe away any residue

To truly sparkle.

The Struggle

To listen to my heart

To bow my ego to my heart

To let the words flow

To allow, to be, to leave alone

To drop, to surrender—

Why, oh why are all these true

And oh so difficult?

What stops me from complete surrender?

Is it because I was taught not to trust life?

Not to trust anyone?

To always watch out for myself?

For the world was out to get me?

I was told everyone knows better

And to do as I was told.

Can years of indoctrination

Melt away in meditation?

Can I break free from the chains of *Samsara*[2]

And surrender to the one true chord?

Can I trust in *Shakti*[3]

And allow her to elevate me?

What do I need to do to achieve such grace?

Or is it that I do not need to do anything anymore?

Like the great poet *Kabir*[4], I pray to one day proclaim,

"Lifting the veil, I have seen the truth."

---

[2] *Samsara* is a concept in Hinduism and Buddhism that refers to the continuous cycle of birth, life, death, and rebirth (reincarnation). It is also known as the cycle of existence or the wheel of life. In Sanskrit, "samsara" means "wandering" or "flowing on."

[3] *Shakti*, is our life force flowing in all of us. Shakti is revered in Hinduism as the di- vine feminine energy and the feminine counterpart to Lord Shiva. Shakti represents the feminine energy in all of us. The yin to yang.

[4] *Kabir Das* was a well-known Indian mystic, poet and saint. He is considered both a Sufi and a Brahmin saint.

Forgive Me, I Failed to Love Myself

Forgive me, Father, for I have sinned.

With a tenderness I have not known, the priest asks, "What is your sin, my child?"

I let myself down,

"How did you do that, my child?"

I never stood up for myself;

I never spoke up for myself;

I spoke up for everyone.

My mother, my sister, even my father

But I never spoke up for myself.

My voice failed me, cracked each time I tried. "Why is that, my child?"

Because I felt I wasn't enough,

Because I felt that everyone would see me as stupid.

They would laugh at me

Because I felt they would not listen.

A grave sin I committed, oh Father.

I have failed myself many a time

Over and over again,

Time and again.

I did not trust myself;

I lost connection to my truth.

I did not trust what I wished for.

My dreams, my hopes, my desires I overlooked.

I dismissed.

I was not strong enough to stand up for them

To stand for my truth

To own my power

To realize my light.

I pushed it all away,

Made an excuse for my silence,

Dismissed my intellect

And each time I scarred,

Each time I ached.

I can no longer take it, oh Father.

What must I do to ease the pain?

How do I forgive myself, Father

For forsaking my own divinity,

For forgetting my connection to God?

How do I let go of this pain?

"My dear child,

You will always be a pure child of the Lord,

No matter what you do.

Love yourself as God loves you.

And forsake all these untruths that you hold close

to your chest,

For they do not serve you.

Understand God's plan for you.

Release the pain that you cling to.

Experience freedom in its release.

Welcome the world with open arms;

Embrace yourself.

You never lost your connection to the divine,

For divinity is you.

Understand your truth;

Smell your musk.

Respect your creation.

Nothing is lost yet

For on your knees, you repent.

Forgive yourself.

Oh, sweet child,

Love yourself

As God loves you."

The Dawn
of Rebirth

*From everything to nothing from nothing to everything,
burned and shredded I surrender to this path of light.
I open my heart and pray to do your bidding.*

My Womb Can Rebirth Me

Was my womb created only to bear children?

Do I have sex energy only for sex?

Or does it serve a higher purpose?

Kundalini energy, the yogis call it.

Healers revere sex energy as food for the brain.

If sex energy is food for the brain,

It can birth many a thing other than a child.

My sex energy can birth my dreams,

My hopes, and my desires.

It can birth my love for the world.

My sex energy can regenerate me,

Grow my brain,

Heal me.

And so a truth I realize—

A truth I knew from long ago.

My womb can birth my dreams

And it can rebirth me.

No Longer Afraid to Stand Alone

I am no longer afraid to stand alone,

To breathe alone,

To live alone.

Isolated or whatever you may call it,

I am no longer afraid if you leave me,

Ignore me or abandon me.

I am not afraid of this world

Or life or what it holds,

For I am a child of the Universe,

Truly a child of the divine.

And this is a return journey home

And with the earth as my family,

I hold no fear in my heart.

I release all anger and all pain.

I no longer engage in the relations that once defined me

As I let go of each chain.

My chest breathes a sigh of relief.

No longer tangled

No longer constrained

And finally free.

Learning to Live

What is this life about?

Is it about living in joy?

What is joy?

Why are we all so serious all the time?

Whatever happened to play?

Why am I so serious about spirituality?

Should not all this bring me joy, happiness and play?

Is it not this that I ultimately seek?

Joy in every breath, every moment, every sleep?

How does one attain this ecstasy?

By stepping lightly

By breathing

By laughing

By walking and living lightly

By not running with the mind

By dancing with the heart

By singing the song of the soul

By embracing silence

By listening.

The "Original" Mind

Oh beautiful mind of mine,

You were once but innocent and unwritten

And then, like a sponge, you started absorbing.

Without discriminating,

Copying and coping,

Losing originality,

Losing imagination,

Your powers buried.

A foe to the heart you became,

Lost in a mirage

A self-created maze

Until it all began to smother.

As silence started to creep in,

You quietened.

You realized devotion.

Mantra and meditation became home.

As you turned around

To journey back to your whole

No longer master

But now a devoted servant,

You bowed down

And humbled in prayer,

Paid homage to your true master:

The heart.

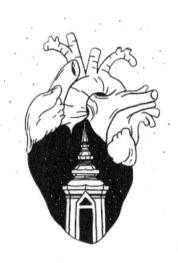

I Am

I will go as I am.

I will return as I am.

And one day soon,

I will realize all that I am.

What Am I to Create?

To create out of nothing

A meaningful something

A chord struck in your soul

A truth revealed

A kiss of truth

A moment of purity

An essence divine

One of a kind

A long forgotten song

A freshness, a newness

A wildness

A wilderness to go through

A life through an hourglass

Timelessness

Nothingness

What am I to create?

"It will come to you," I receive.

A Code Decrypted

Butterflies flutter;

Birds fly.

Conversations flower—

I relish in solitude.

A love true—

True to my soul.

A love of my truth—

My truth revealed.

An insanity—

A sanity found.

A loss for words—

I do not write; I flow.

A necessity achieved,

A world of energy.

Things unseen, unheard,

None of the world makes sense.

And yet it all finally fits.

The meaning revealed,

The Mona Lisa decrypted.

A code understood

A voice heard

A song sung.

Reflections on the Buddha

Their jewels mean nothing, their positions wisps of air.

Ready to forsake all for a glimpse of the eternal truth

as seen by the Supreme Buddha.

Buddha was one of us,

A human born from a woman's womb.

And so it is

That the eternal spark of wisdom rests in each of us

And waits to be touched, to be felt, to be seen,

to be heard.

And once it is found, there is no struggle

For all suffering continues and yet it ends

As a new wisdom takes light, takes shape

As wings of eternity burst forth.

There is no striving;

There is only thriving.

For so the one truth stands

That there is no bigger task at hand

Than to work on the inner aura, inner wisdom

To grow in meditation, in love

To let go in compassion

To let go of all that no longer serves

To let go of it all.

For it is only in letting go

That true freedom is found.

Devotion

Through the sands of time,

She has sprung forth like a fountain of faith.

Into the unknown she dances

With strength, courage and vigor.

Love in her heart, her soul, her bones,

She knew not what true love was

Until she saw the universe in her eyes.

She knew not that faith and love were intertwined,

until she tried to seek one ignoring the other.

And it is no ordinary kind of love for her God

that she seeks;

It is an unconditional love.

The love that Prabhav's heart felt for *Lord Vishnu*[5],

For which he denied his father, his family.

So in devotional love was Prabhav lost

That neither fire nor hate could hurt or harm him

And so she learns that true devotion to God

Is but a path of unconditional love

And her soul thirsts to touch the depths of such devotion for the Supreme

So that she too might be worth

Of a sigh or a smile from the Creator.

And alas no other love can or ever will fill her cup,

For she will soon be home

For eternity.

---

5 *Lord Vishnu* is a Hindu deity who is considered the Lord of preservation. In this story a young boy Prabhav forsakes his family for the love of Lord Vishnu.

Oneness

The buffalo looks into my eyes.

The lizard stares at the tree.

The five elements speak to me—

Earth, fire, water, air, ether.

All a composition of my DNA

And no difference do I see

Between the buffalo, the lizard and me.

Mother Earth's Wisdom to Her Child

A message from Mother Earth

Live naturally, she sings through the birds

Breathe, she whispers in the wind

Live in joy, the tree hugs me

Laugh and live and live and laugh

Look at all my other children

From the birds to the worms to the noisy cricket

to the mightiest lion.

Look at how they move

With calm strength

With laughter in their steps,

For they all know, that one day they will return to me

As will you, my child.

Enjoy the journey

It was never about the destination

It has always been about the steps—

One in front of the other

A breath at a time

Rejoice in the splendor of your life

Contentment is joy.

Dance like your soul is all there is

For that is all there is

Let your spirit sing my songs in joy

Ahuewe, my child, Ahuewe.

Ancient words and songs say it all

You know the truth for you breathe it all

Young or old, the leaf will fall

Death knows not age or race.

And until your clock is up,

Laugh, my child, oh laugh

Live in joy, each breath in joy

There is nothing much to this existence

Except to live in joy

And so I say to you as your mother

Until the day you return to eternally rest in my bosom

Until then, oh sweet child of mine.

Sing like the birds;

dance like the bamboo

Run like the fox

Fear nothing

And love everything.

I Am the Key and the Key Is Me

Divine timing.

There is no such thing, my mind said.

Plan and execute.

No! my heart said.

Let us trust.

Yes! My heart cried.

And for the first time,

I trusted the rhythm of my heart.

I trusted when it told me to let go of certainty,

To embrace the unknown

Even if only for a day

And the miracles unfolded.

Feeding the monks, I felt blessed with good karma.

I teared up, for I never realized that I had good karma,

Never gave myself credit enough, kindness enough,

love enough.

I connected with the human race in the most

beautiful way.

A smile, a gesture, a hug—

Love needs no language.

A random stranger offered a ride

And it all unfolded

Like magic.

The key to the temple in my hand

As I witnessed the power of people's faith

many a century ago—

The key lies within me;

I am the key and the key is me.

And as long as I follow this brave beautiful heart

of mine,

I will forever be happy

Because I will forever be true

To me.

The Silence Within

Where is the silence that I so desperately seek?

My being cringes at the sounds of the outside world—

People's voices, the sounds of humans,

The cars, the crowd, the music.

Oh it throbs my head and aches my heart.

Silence, I seek you.

God, I seek you.

Where are you?

A part of me wonders

The eternal stillness, the quiet

That I seek outside.

Is that not inside

The stillness that I must nurture

The flower that I must nourish?

Is that not within me?

The silence is within.

The eternal depths of solitude,

The infinite nothingness

All lie inside,

So close and yet out of reach.

What if I chose to focus on the silence inside

instead of outside?

Would the noise outside affect me so?

What if I chose to focus only on my internal silence

To grow it

To soil it To feed it?

How do I allow my internal silence to surface?

How do I connect with it?

Breathe;

Go within.

You are close.

Be quiet in your mind—

In your heart

In your breath

In your attitude

In your step.

With each breath, be only in the now.

Yes, it may disappoint,

But when did I tell you that this path is easy?

You are being tested.

You are meant to put into practice what you have
studied.

Keep the silence within;

Grow the silence inside.

Light the flame—

The eternal flame of God.

Spirit cannot exist without material.

Emotions cannot exist without the physical.

Like four wheels of a car, they all must move together.

If one falters, each falters.

And in all this, do not forget to pray and to play.

It is not a quest; it is a journey.

It is not a fight; it is a meditation.

A walking, living, breathing meditation.

Let each moment be your medicine;

Let each breath be your guide.

Be so engulfed in the present moment.

Not for a breath, let your mind falter.

The past is but a calendar;

The future only exists in a date.

Neither is a reality,

But the now,

The eternal now—

It is all there is.

Practice your silence in the now

By embracing your inner stillness.

Let nothing outside affect your inside.

This is the practice that you must do.

Let nothing on the outside, good or bad,

happy or sad

Affect your inside.

Equanimity, serenity

A breath of eternity

A silence so divine

Not a storm could interrupt

so human sounds hold

no face

A silence so pure

That none can corrupt

A silence so golden

Connected to the Universe.

Connect to this divinity within;

You are silence.

Walk into it, embrace it, own it,

Breathe it, love it.

Witness it.

Witness your breath.

Witness the turmoil.

Listen inwards.

Listen to the golden silence within.

Do not fear anymore.

Do not run anywhere.

Face it.

Connect to your inner silence.

That is the silence that beseeches you.

The outside does not matter;

The outside never mattered.

Connect to the silence inside.

That is your heart's desire.

You vowed to follow your heart

And so follow your heart you must.

Connect to your inner silence;

Therein lies the wisdom you seek.

Answers multifold peace boundless

Connect to the silence within.

Therein is your key.

Your dreams and hopes,

Your clarity—

Connect to the silence within,

For there, you shall find me

Waiting for you, oh dear child.

Connect to your silence within

And have a taste of eternity.

A Fear of Death or Never Having Lived?

My heart races at the thought of death.

One day, one moment, it will all come to an end.

All hopes and desires over,

All dreams dead and gone.

Loved ones departed or apart

And yet I live as though I'm immortal.

The thought that I would never again

See the sea or hear the birds

A lump catches in my throat

That I would never laugh nor love

Or be loved pains me.

So much attachment to this life I have

And yet I question, Do I live it?

Or does the shadow of death

Push me to live so hard

To laugh each day until tears spring forth?

And my tummy aches with love

To love so much until my heart explodes

To grow and to treat all beings seen and unseen

with tenderness and compassion

To paint rainbows for children

To tickle the old

To squeeze each bit of happiness out of life

Before it is too late

And before this story ends.

My Hands

I stare at my hands, a lifetime of plans

And I wonder what memories they store.

If they could speak what tales, would they yield

Of truth or bitter told?

Are they proud of the deeds done, the life lived

The seeds sown, the fruits reaped

The memories breathed

The prayers said?

Are my hands grateful,

Or do they feel remorse

Or worse

Reject me?

If my hands could speak,

What stories would they tell?

What Is This Life I Wonder?

What is this life? I wonder.

Birth to death, death to birth

A paradox of choices

A myriad of decisions

Continuous questions

Endless hopes

Flowing desires

Guilt, fear, anxiety

Everyday friends

Laughter, joy, play

Sought after guests

But must it be so

Must those welcome guests be sought after

And those nasties be friends?

What would happened if there were

A day where laughter, joy and play were the norm

And guilt, fear, anxiety had no score?

Rejected and dejected they would leave

What if life translated into a joyful melody?

Where would that leave worry?

Can life be lived simply

No worry, fear or dejection

Absolute and whole

Pure and in love?

This is the life I desire

And this is the life I create.

Bliss

Such a joy arises,

Familiar yet unfamiliar.

A smile grows from inside out.

A cup of tea rejoices.

Chocolate food for the soul.

I have stopped in time.

Or has time stopped for me?

The world I see different

A song for my ears only.

Suddenly everywhere is beauty—

A friendly smile

A laugh

A bird

The sea.

My heart plays a tune.

For the first time unafraid.

Is this what it means to be in the moment?

To write like a pianist

To walk like a dancer

To smile from inside out—

I feel alive

And bliss.

Guilt-free, I relish

A treat so divine

To not worry

To laugh at my idiosyncrasies.

It is a joyful life,

Each moment a present

A sweet to be unwrapped,

A hug waiting an embrace.

A lover's kiss

A wisp of cloud

It is good to be alive

To breathe

And feel the cool breeze.

What a joy to be alive

To truly be alive.

Life Force

To live in equanimity

To see all as me and me in all

To see God in every creature large or small—

Is it a task too big?

A mission impossible?

Or a revolutionary act of lifting the false curtain?

For is this not the eternal truth?

Are we not all part of that one life force

That runs through each of us?

However you name it,

The same energy that courses the veins of the plants

And the leaves of the trees

The sinews of animals

And the pulse of the birds,

Do not we all share the same life force

That rests in an acorn?

And so it now makes sense

That I sometimes see my mischievousness

in a cat's eyes

Or hear my song in a bird's melody

Or feel warmth in the hug of a tree.

For we are all one

And one in all are we.

A Shifting

Paradigms are shifting;

Clocks are turning.

Wheels are churning,

Fate revolving.

A new tide arriving

Finally descending

A plethora of loving

An era of serving

Of selfless giving

Of detached living.

Faith

Faith.

A non-imposing all-encompassing five letter word:

Faith.

How do I practice?

Detach myself from outcome,

Trust that the same infinite wisdom that guides birds to worms, fish to food, brings shelter to the forgotten, will guide me, protect me, nourish me and provide for me.

And so it is.

But why?

Why is it so difficult to believe?

To trust

To trust the unseen with utmost certainty in its power and its magic?

Why?

Why is it so difficult?

To let things flow and simply be

Why?

Why is it so difficult to let go, to allow, to be?

A Thirst for Wings

I always wished to be a bird.

The thought of wings to sail the world

Would bring a smile to my lips and a spring to my step

To soar the skies endlessly with not a care,

not a thought, not a burden

Light weight and airy

To chirp and twist in the air and play

amongst my fellow birds

To rise at dawn and sing my heart out and bask

my wings in the sun's rays

To return at dusk murmuring with my mates

as we exchanged the day's stories

To rise to the sky, to soar boundlessly,

To dive and to dance to an inner tune.

But maybe, just maybe, I am a bird,

A bird of my own kind,

A bird who thought she lost her wings,

or worse that her wings were cut off

And suddenly she found her wings.

You see,

I always had wings;

I was born with wings.

I simply forgot until the twists and turns of life

and the callings of my soul reminded me that I need

not have ever held any envy for the winged creatures

of the sky, for like them, I was created with my own

wings.

Somehow, they got closed before they were opened

until one day my wings could no longer stay closed.

And I woke up to find that I too could fly.

I too could rise at dawn and soar the sky.

I too could retreat at sunset bountiful and gay.

So yes, my wish did come true.

For I have found my wings that are stronger

than the strongest

And that will carry me to many a distant land

And yet always bring me home.

The Compass

Connect with the root of your roots,

Your source your inner truth.

Embark on the journey within

The journey that was always there.

Are these just words

Or do they have weight?

What are my roots?

I know as I know the air I breathe that there

is an inner knowing

Like *Vasilisa's* little doll[6] that guided her to safety.

I too have an inner doll.

Some call it intuition;

I call it my compass,

My ever faithful navigator.

What if I gave up on the little self entirely,

Stopped listening to the mind

And only tuned inwards to my intuition,

to my doll

What would happen?

Shall I try it today?

---

6 *Vasilisa* the Beautiful is a Russian fairy tale. When Vasilisa's mother was dying she gave her a doll to keep with her wherever she went. As the story goes Vasilisa's doll guided her to safety.

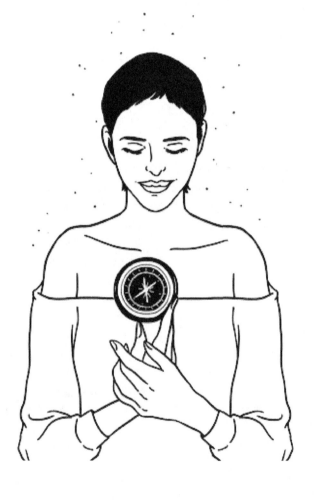

Forever Free

A timeless realization that I can only depend on myself

for my happiness

No other, nothing outside, nothing in this world

Can bring me happiness

And so I gift myself happiness

This realization is my birthday gift to myself,

worth more than diamonds and gold

No matter what or who shows up outside

in whatsoever shape or form

I can choose how I feel inside

I can choose to light a candle

Or enter a dark tunnel

I am powerful, commanding and royal

As royal as the wolf into whose blue eyes and warm fur

I once melted

I embrace the creator and the creation

And I can choose how to react in each moment

no matter what that moment may hold

It is all up to me

Because inside I have always been free.

Do Not Dishonor Yourself

Keep writing.

Keep writing.

What do you wish for me to write?

Please

Guide me.

I am ready to listen.

Keep writing.

What should I write?

Your soul—

The insides of your soul

The depths of your ether

Your buried treasures.

Do everything different;

Break all patterns.

Do not dishonor yourself even for one second.

Embrace who you are,

Who you always were,

Who you were meant to be.

Honor your guidance.

She only seeks your truth.

For without this,

You do not live but merely float

And to live is for each cell,

Each element inside you to form

the perfect composition,

The perfect melody,

A unison undefined and one that can only

be experienced.

And it is that to which you must return

And so write.

Keep writing

Until you arrive.

Effortless Existence

In a trance I am.

As these words pour from a place I did not know

until now,

I know that I must continue.

I feel the embers rising to my chest,

A calmness and yet an urgency.

The paradoxes continue

And this time I allow each of them

to show me the light.

I trust what is happening.

I trust it with my soul.

I trust with the depths of the many lives

that my soul has lived

And will continue to live.

Immortal I am.

Limited and yet unlimited in a mortal body

Sans time sans space.

I breathe; I live.

For what is death without birth?

And what if there is no birth

But instead an enchanting cycle of growth

Of elevation

Of regeneration

Of liberty

Of vastness

Of ultimate prosperity?

What if we were to remove the confines of birth

and death entirely

And only and simply to be?

To be

Beautiful energy

For is not every molecule of our body if broken down

simply that

Our composition that of the stars

And they do not limit themselves by boxing

into birth and death.

They simply shine.

Even when some die, they shine.

And even those that disappear into the black hole,

I am certain end up somewhere,

Shining.

So is there anything to be really afraid of in this life?

What is there to fear?

Is it not all unfolding in a beautiful composition

That if we were to wake up and finally live the magic

Everything would fleet effortlessly?

And yet we make living such an effortful occupation

But is it really?

Our breath, our digestion, our nervous system

Every system and cell in our body functions

Effortlessly

It does what it needs to do each day.

And yet we decide that we need to make everything

about hard work.

We applaud those who seem to do a million things

And cast away the simpletons.

But perhaps the simpletons have got it right.

Is that the reason they are left bright?

The magic is that there is magic.

It is here.

If only we were to awake from this spell

that we cast on ourselves

And see

That all we are here to do

Is to be alive and rejoice

Until the next stage—

Whatever that might be.

?

If I can imagine anything, what would it be?

If I can be anything, what would I be?

Light

A formlessness

A white light

Infinite time

Timelessness

A death

And yet a deathlessness.

Head Bowed to Heart, I Listen

Let the heart see what the eyes cannot.

Let the heart hear what the ears cannot.

Let the heart feel what the skin cannot.

Let this be my prayer each day

And let me live each breath

With my head bowed to my heart.

What If Your Happily Ever After Is Right Now?

What if your happily ever after is right now?

Happening in this second

In this moment?

What if there is no other time?

There is only now.

After all, is it not true that every moment where

your lips curved up or your tears fell down

Was now?

What if this is all we will ever know or ever have?

What if there is no past or future?

After all, did not they all take place now?

The Ultimate Journey

To connect with the original mind

The mind of God

The mind of Source

The mind of Creation,

Is this not our ultimate journey?

What then is reality?

The fine lines between dreams or what we call dreams

and the real world or what we call the real world

are blurring.

No longer can I tell which from which,

For I feel that neither is real but all the while real.

An odd confusion that never before did exist

A timeless question arising in my depths

As I seek and search to reconnect with my reality,

My truth,

The universal truth.

Are the material goals that we are taught to seek

a reality?

Competition infiltrates our mind at a tender age.

Our innocence eroded and, in its place,

a false pride instilled

With the pride, a false fear too finds company.

Hand in hand, they pull us through life.

First school, then work, then family.

All the while a voice, now tiny, nags

This is not your path.

This is not you.

Break the clutches of the norm;

Break free and return to your truth.

So that you may realize your ultimate potential—

Your ultimate truth far greater than any that you

perceive to be true.

Return to your original state.

Go home and greet the Source.

It is waiting for you.

What Is Yoga?

What is yoga?

A pose, a mantra, a meditation

Lululemons[7], Manduka[8] mats

Breathing techniques

Or so much more?

Patanjali[9] describes yoga as stilling the fluctuations of the mind

Yogananda[10] speaks of yoga as scientific methods of reuniting the soul with the Spirit

The wise words of these great teachers resound- yoga is much more than downward dog and sun salutations

Yoga is the essence of being

The lifting of the veil from duality to non- duality

The ultimate key to freedom.

So what then is yoga?

A map for the lost,

A compass for the forgotten,

An unconditional friend.

A faithful companion,

An ever-loving consort,

A warmth,

A promise of union with the divine,

The Creator of All Things.

An ultimate promise,

A never-ending test,

A knot of love,

The key to freedom,

An acceptance of the whole.

---

7 A yoga and activewear brand.

8 A brand that specializes in yoga related products such as mats and blocks.

9 *Patanjali* was a Hindu author and philosopher and writer of the famous Yoga Sutras.

10 *Paramahansa Yogananda* was a Hindu spiritual teacher who taught many Kriya Shakti. He is the author of the famous book Autobiography of a Yogi.

Who Is to Say What Came First?

As dusk falls and another day bids adieu

And night strolls in and brings

with it the glimmering moon

Day going into night, night going into day,

Who is to say which came first?

A transition flawless, timeless,

Eternal and infinite.

Birth and death we witness each day.

With the rising sun and the graceful moon

And yet we do not see

That we are too but a cycle of this nature.

We breathe in and we breathe out.

A cell is born; a cell dies.

And a time will come when we are no more.

And who knows where we may transition

So who is to say what came first, birth or death,

I wonder.

A Prayer

Hands in prayer,

I bow my head in submission,

Submission to that inner fire within.

The same reflected in the sun

I pray.

I pray for guidance on this journey

Guidance to the truth.

I pray that I recognize who I am.

I pray I have my heart always open.

I pray that my talents continue to flow but how

can I think of shortage when I belong to the infinite

The ever abundant divine?

I pray for prosperity, for health, for truth.

I recognize that I create my universe in this life

and the after

And my life here is reflected in the after.

Somehow this makes sense.

It makes sense to me that I create my own heaven

and hell.

It makes sense to me that I am the creator of my fate.

These hands that I gaze upon have power.

My thoughts and words hold energy—

Energy to create or energy to destroy.

I choose

And I choose, hope.

I choose humility and bow my head down to my heart.

For I know the path to the truth is through my heart

I am grateful for this journey of self-discovery;

I am grateful for the blessings.

The blessing to see, to feel, to realize

To wake up

To allow

To flow

To eternity.

Separation

A sadness from a separation

I did not want to come here.

Even before I was conceived,

I knew I did not want to come here.

I was separated from my source,

Thrown into a jungle of wants and desires,

But is it that I did not want to come

Or is it that I chose to come but the separation

of sadness lives on?

An ultimate separation from my source

From oneness

I know what the words mean, but my being says it is

a pain deeper than that which words can ascribe to.

The all-encompassing *Om*[11],

The sound of the universe or perhaps God.

The *Vedas*[12] an ancient text have my answers

And yet the ultimate wisdom is revealed

by the *Upanishads*[13].

The ultimate light rests inside each of us,

Waiting silently, watching us hoping that

it is realized in this lifetime.

I feel utterly confused today.

I feel my life is not my life.

I feel none of it is mine.

Do I even own anything?

The garments, my home, my car, the gold snake ring

I bought the other day, this body?

I am not sure of any of this anymore.

I feel like retiring into a nest.

Becoming a hermit for a while sounds heavenly.

Perhaps I can live in a cottage in the wilderness?

Or escape to a black hole?

---

11 *Om*, a sacred sound considered by ancient texts to be the sound of the universe.

12 *Vedas*, ancient religious texts originating in ancient India.

13 *Upanishads*, ancient texts of wisdom originating after the Vedas in India.

Death Trance

Once a thriving human,

Now nothing more than a corpse.

As breathing humans danced in prayer above,

A family completed the final rites for their

loved one below.

Adorned to the last second,

Only to be burned to ashes.

Transfixed, as though planted in cement, I looked on

My being not wanting to move.

Enchanted, entranced in wonder

In wonder as to the fickleness of life

In wonder as to the emptiness of it all.

Nothing left.

Not even our bodies.

And what a grand spectacle we parade during

our lifetimes.

And even funerals a galore of grandeur.

Why so much fuss for a shell?

The essence long gone

The person who was no longer there

How many did he hurt?

Who did he hurt?

How many did he love?

Who loved him in turn?

Did it all matter?

Does it all matter?

If we are all going to die one day.

My mortality, I question.

Hypnotized by the cremation,

The smell of burning corpses somehow a conciliation

A deep-seated humbling

Not a sadness but a reckoning

The ashes of death an addictive drug

of the last remnants of a human life

The funeral rites complete.

The men shave their hair.

I thought shaving was a sign of new beginnings.

So is death but a new beginning?

For how long do the living grieve the dead?

And what of nature that is in constant evolution?

In a constant cycle of life and death and birth

and rebirth?

What of that?

Why then do we grieve the dead?

Their memory nothing but an attachment,

An oasis in the desert, a façade.

Why do we grieve their loss?

Do we grieve for them or do we grieve for us?

When Dad died, I cried.

I cried because I somehow felt guilty,

Guilty for not having spent enough time with him,

Guilty for not being there.

Did he feel guilty?

Perhaps once he passed on

But during his life, he lived his way.

Rejoiced in his aloneness and his state of mind

So did I cry for his loss?

Or did I cry for my ego?

Why do we grieve the dead?

Do we really miss their presence?

Or do we miss what they gave or could give us?

Do we care much for each other at all?

Or do we each want our egos to be fed?

Is it because we are all so thirsty for love

So terribly hungry like ghouls to be seen, to be heard,

to be loved?

Is it that our separation from our Source

at birth was so severe

That our hunger for love never seems to disappear

Unless we embark on a spiritual path

Whatever that path may be?

To find a way, a path, a route back to our source

Does that not make death our greatest teacher.

For now that we see and know that we have an
unknown end

Should we not use this life to strive to our creator?

Should we not connect with our inner powers

our gifts bestowed to connect with the fire

The fire that is burning in each of us?

The light that is aching to shine out of us

Should we not focus entirely on this single goal

of union, of oneness?

Why is it so hard?

Why is it so hard to live?

Or is it

Is life not just one breath at a time

With no record or guarantee of the next?

Clearly death is the greatest teacher,

For are we not mortal immortal beings

or immortal mortal beings?

With frail bodies but steadfast spirits

Should we not spend more time exercising our spirits

than working out our bodies?

We grieve at death while we should grieve

if we are dead while awake

For is it not a blessing to be alive and to experience

this world

And to soldier on in our inner journeys?

Why wait until death to understand life?

Why not understand life while it beats?

The Feminine Is Birthing

The feminine is birthing.

She wants to love and be loved.

She wants to caress and be caressed.

Tender yet strong are her steps.

She flows; she sways to her own magic.

Wisps of cloud float around her.

Butterflies shy from her beauty,

Graceful, yet flirty.

A budding flower, she emerges.

A goddess of purity,

Immense is her love.

For all creatures large and small, seen and unseen,

She awaits in her glory.

A golden light floats around her.

The swivel of her hips,

The heave in her breasts,

Her sexuality she boasts.

No longer shy of her desires

All of which she owns.

Her skin too small to contain her,

Her body constrains her,

For she is bursting

And wishes to envelope the world in her arms

In her beauty

In her tender kisses

And she is ready to receive love

From her masculine

A divine union she anticipates.

And confidently, she awaits,

For with or without her mate

She knows her skin,

And in her being,

she finds plentiful cups of love

A tenderness, a joy.

In earth, she merges

Everywhere and nowhere.

The feminine can no longer be contained.

In her right, she sustains,

For she knows the world has long been waiting

her arrival

And today she arrives,

Quiet and bold.

Beautiful in gold,

She arrives.

We Are the Light That We Seek

Unexplored talents, unspoken gifts

We float around this life

With our burdens in grit.

It is as though we vow to forget the original contracts

we once made.

We look the other way to society and nod yes

to all it takes.

A wise woman once whispered,

"Toss the security blanket."

What false sense of security do we seek, in society,

in family, in culture, in religion

For is it not all a façade

A speck of man's creation

A product of imagination?

What is the love, understanding and acceptance

we crave?

Is this not a need to be fulfilled only by divine grace?

But the paradox remains.

We cannot embrace divine grace with hands

full of material gain.

Detachment to all a precondition to eternal love

And so the climax of our lives

We spend half our lives accumulating

And the other half learning to let go

And pondering the question who am I? Why am I here.

We wander the streets of life.

Sometimes we see a ray of light as another acknowl-
edges our gift.

Excited, we rejoice, "I have found my gift,"

Only to later succumb to melancholy

And feed the lower demons who hang on desperately.

And so we succumb and feed the creatures

of self-doubt and self-loathing

And once again move further from our gift

from our creation.

Again, we wander the lonely streets

And darkness soon descends.

But just as darkness engulfs,

an unexpected light ascends.

As we look outside in awe to find the source

of this light,

Where does this beautiful, serene light emanate from?

We ponder.

Not pausing to consider

Or stopping to see

That the light we despair for

Is shining brightly from within,

For we are the flame that we seek.

.

The Rising

It is time to not be afraid of my light,
It is time to be brave to be bold in my truth,
It is time to shine brighter than I ever shone,
It is time to rise.

The Wild and the Woman Unite

I let everything go.

I surrendered it all for her one true embrace.

The identity that I thought defined me

The roles that I thought gave my existence meaning

The possessions that I thought gave my breath power

The recognition that I thought made my heart beat.

Piece by piece, layer by layer, heavy like armor,

I unburdened.

Surrendered. Bare. Nothing. No one.

Attached no more to a job

Attached no more to a role

Attached no more to recognition

Attached no more to praise—

I lay bare,

Stripped and standing alone,

Anchored alone in my faith.

With nothing to keep me warm on a cold winter's day

But there she came

With the kindest blue eyes and a hint of amber in each
burning bright

Her steps purposeful, commanding and royal.

For no ordinary wolf she was

As she wrapped herself around my bare body

I was born.

My core touched by her wild nature

And yet no stranger to her urgent call awoke

the long-slain fire burning in the pit of my uterus,

For I was giving birth to myself in a way that

no mother gave birth to a son.

Eruptions of wild ambers, unearthed desires,

gifts unleashed.

It had been too long in the waiting,

My spine erect,

My shoulders straightened.

Neck high,

Head to the sky,

I walked on

With nothing, but everything.

She was awake inside of me.

And it was time.

It was time to not be afraid of my own light.

It was time to not be afraid to be seen, to be heard,

to be bold, to be brave in my truth.

To shun the definitions of society and to create

my own,

As we reunited in this vessel of mine growing higher

and higher like a phoenix ascending to the sun,

Magic

Pure magic.

As we took alight, no longer divided and each fighting

a different war but now one—the wild and the woman

united,

Our mission, a simple yet complex one.

To be truth

To live in truth

To break away and pull away from the ashes that have

clouded our truth, over and over again,

time and time again

To wipe away the dust from our eyes and see

our truth in light

For there are no limits

And even if bare and with no clothes,

and no flesh and only bones

There I am and there you will find me shining brighter

and brighter than ever before

Brighter than I ever shone

For I am an undefeatable and indomitable light

and a light that none can touch, take, or steal

Forever bright, forever true, forever burning.

My Voice

My gift to the world I know

Is my voice,

The melody, the sound that

Passes my soft lips

The gentle hum

The vibration in my chords

The sound from the depths of my soul

The words that escape

Harm or love,

Love more than harm

Admittedly sometimes cause more harm.

Why the harm?

Is rage not my right as is love?

To let the pain escape my soul when I have been

wronged to the depths of my being,

Am I not to hold to the truth of the pain and cry

when it hurts deeper than a knife slicing a bone?

To shout, to scream, to yell, to behave—

what they term unladylike?

Why are there dos and don'ts in the way that I speak

when every baby that is born first cries to the top

of its lungs whether it is a boy or a girl, it matters not.

Why am I to hold my rage down deep until it boils

and churns and spreads into a cancerous venom

Until I cannot contain it, and it turns me blue

and sick?

When a simple release would heal me,

I am told to stay shut and seal me.

Is it because I am a woman?

Do body parts define the shackles that are placed

on me?

I am sorry. Please excuse me. I did not mean that—

is this to be my only vocabulary?

Does it progress the world for me to hold shut and

to behave in a way that they accept at all times

with no pardon?

Am I to be gentle always and not let the waters shake

and the barriers break?

And so what if they did?

Would it be so bad?

Would I be shunned more than I already am?

Because I am a woman?

Is my voice less than when it is more than?

Is it that my voice is taken feeble?

I do not mean harm.

But I need release.

I need to be heard; my soul no longer can be contained

by the falsities it is told to confine by.

As rightful as a newborn's cry or a sparrow's song

or a lion's roar,

No amount of shutting up or sealing down

can constrain my voice, which even if I try,

It does not heed for my voice is often my betrayer,

Gifted as I may be at masking the pain behind a smile,

my voice often escapes the barricades I place as it

flaunts to the world my fears, my doubts, my sarcasm.

I try to regain composure, I breathe, I go on,

Walking the stage of life

To perform yet another act, another scene.

Politically correct, you should.

Why I ask?

Who decided what is and is not politically correct?

And why am I not allowed to trust the sound that

spurns and rises from my sinews and my very depths

And reverberates with joy each time I speak

in harmony to the heartbeat of the earth?

How can I not trust that sound?

Trust that sound more, much more than what you

tell me to be.

And yet the answer I get to all my questions always

is the same,

An old adage that few have challenged to date

Because the world was made this way, I am told.

By who? I ask.

By you and me.

An Everlasting Union

When the sands of time

Turn yet another page

Of divinity, of love, of power Of faith and of fate,

A love profound awakens

A joy untold unfolds

As 12 petals open

And 972 unfold.

An everlasting union awaits

An eternity of purity and gold.

My Soul Is Dancing

My soul is dancing,

Finally alight.

Music fills my heart.

My feet hover.

I dance like the palm trees in the wind.

No longer tied,

I sail to the highest mountain.

A flight on the wings of the Almighty,

A sacred spirit rises within me—

One that I cannot control

And so I surrender

To the wind, the fire, the earth, the water

And to the spirit,

Unconcerned about the destination

About the time or the situation,

For all that matters is

My soul is dancing

Finally alight.

Desert Flower

A woman's life is akin to that of a desert—

A desert,

Misunderstood, misinterpreted, underestimated.

Life on a desert is concentrated.

Much of it occurs underground

Much like that of a woman's.

The desert by nature is neither lush nor rich

like its forest relative,

But yet it contains within it the mysteries

and the secrets of life concentrated on it.

Many a woman has lived a desert life.

Small on the surface, enormous under the ground

From my grandmother to my mother to name a few

Their psyches damned to that of a desert

Suppression, limitation, expectation

All of which a burden none of which their choosing.

Life's cruelties aghast

And so she believes she cannot ask.

She cannot dream a life larger than what she knows.

She cannot conceive a life above ground.

Choked, caught in the sands of time,

unaware of the quicksand, the sucking dry

The lack of water, the shape shifting oasis.

She continues.

Unaware that she is being boned dry,

Boned dry from the expectations,

from the views of life that are not her own

and only serve to chisel at her spirit

And so she lives, believing that there

is only one cactus with one flower,

But if she were to venture further

Just a little further for a little longer,

Perhaps the shape shifting oasis may be real after all

Perhaps there exists a reality that surpasses

her wildest dreams

If only she would venture a little further

for a little longer

Undeterred by the terrain, by the merciless sun,

by the burning sand, crawl through the canyons,

battle the scorpions.

Only a little further, a few steps more,

a few breaths more,

There she would find on the other side

Her oasis awaiting her

Her transformation

Her dreams, her shackles broken.

No longer constrained, no longer concentrated

No longer one cactus or one flower

But a garden in full bloom.

A well of water

An abundance of spirit—

If only she would venture

A few more steps for just a little longer.

A Faithful Love

Every step of the way

At each age

In each moment in time

My constant companion, a faithful love

Words of all the great ones who came before

Sad and lonely, I open a page.

Maya Angelou wraps me in her arms

And says, "Do not whine; do not complain,

Change your attitude; breathe again."

Afraid of tomorrow and regretting yesterday,

Eckhart Tolle takes my hand.

"Be here now", he says. "The present is all there is."

Time and time again, words have proven

my one loyal friend

A life jacket, a warm cup of tea, a blanket on a cold day

And when my heart has sung its song,

I have turned to whirling Rumi

And he has promised

"Out beyond ideas of wrongdoing and right doing

there is a field. I'll meet you there."

And when my soul has danced its tune,

The humble poet Kabir's words have struck the tune,

"Listen to me, my friend! My beloved Lord is within."

And so I castaway the grim.

I unload the weight of the world.

I whirl in Rumi's grace

And love like Kabir's faith,

For I too am a child of God

United in God's embrace.

I Honor My Song

A bird not a kite I wish to be.

No master will control my destiny.

With wings, I soar

And travel to distant lands

To my heart's galore,

For there is a song in my heart

That must be sung

To honor my creation.

I cannot and will not let it die within me.

Such disservice shall not be done.

I owe it to the world,

And just like the bird sings its song,

Whether or not anyone listens,

I too sing my song.

Whether or not it is heard,

I sing it for my heart, my soul and for divinity.

Let It All Explode in Me

Let all the portals open.

Let all the gates fly wide.

Heaven, hell

Dark lights and white lights

Effervescent lights

Galaxies, nebulae

Planets, black holes

The sun, the moon

The core of the earth

Let it all explode in me.

It Is Time to Rise

To open your body

Like a blossoming flower

To move in a way neither gentle nor cute

But true to your feminine desire

To connect to your wild nature

Fire ablaze

Constraints aghast

Free in your own skin

To breathe for the first time

Wild woman now that is me.

Unapologetic, fierce

A fountain of love

A vessel of divine sexuality

Taboos abreast,

The goddess rises.

True to her sword,

Her words alight, she takes flight.

Higher and higher evolving

Effervescent light

Paths aligned

It is time

For the rivers to burst forth

For the love to spring forth

For time to stand still

For the divine feminine to rise

No longer still

No longer quiet

It is time to speak up.

Silence no longer serves

This heart of mine

Which is bold and brave.

Bare breasted, I stroll the roads

No longer afraid of my power.

It is time to own me

Time to love me

Time to caress and to touch me

Time to hug and to love me

It is time to conquer myself

No longer hiding

Open and brave

Flowing and true to my soul.

The inner goddess rises

To shine and to reclaim.

It is time

To rise.

Does It End?

Crying and screaming

Fighting to be let out

Dissolving

Rejuvenating

Falling, rising

Rising, falling

Tears

Laughter

Pain

Anger

Rage

Love

Does it end?

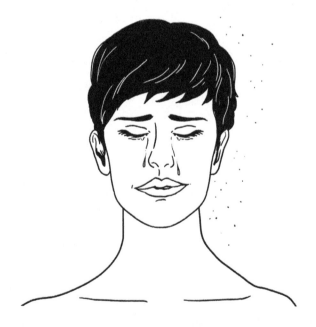

The Forgotten Feminine

The feminine rejects nothing.

She receives.

Indiscriminate to gender,

She co-exists in humble companion with the masculine.

Resident in all of us, be it man, woman or child,

She flows

And yet society permeates the masculine

So that the feminine is forgotten.

The receiving

The tenderness

The gentle flow

Delicate steps

A humble glow

All forgotten for linear thinking.

Strategic accounting

Fast moving

Snap deciding

Tough frontiers

Rigid exteriors

And yet she emerges

Slowly flowing

Making her way through.

She permeates the impermeable,

Gently nudging us, saying,

Remember me

I am love and without me, you cannot exist.

So come with me

And see your glories manifold.

See your heart's true desires.

Relish your gold.

Because Today I Breathe

Oh magical and elegant moon,

The dark night's saving grace.

Enchanting and powerful

From so far in the skies

Unafraid to shine bright

Unconcerned, unbothered

Reflecting the waters

Enchanting the skies

A silver trance

A grateful dance

A cooling embrace

A touch of the soul

Deep within, lie all the answers.

Angel wings I see in the clouds

My fate coming to life

All is being revealed.

All will be revealed.

All I must do is trust

And experience it all with open arms,

an open mind and an open heart.

Why?

Because today I breathe.

A Mantra from Within

A mantra from within—

I am my own calm.

I am my own center.

I am my own silence.

I am my own question.

I am my own answer.

Each Special and Unique

The squirrel does not look to the bird and wish to fly.

It carries on, plays, lives its life.

The butterfly does not look to the bee and wish

to make honey.

It dances from flower to flower and grows

more flowers.

But as humans, we do not follow nature.

We compare.

We contrast.

We judge.

We envy.

Where do all these low emotions originate?

Each of us a chord of the divine

And the divine only knows love.

So why do we spend our precious energy

on these dark feelings?

Why not blend with divinity, submerge into love?

And see the beauty that each of us brings to the world

Like the squirrel, the bird, the butterfly, the bee

All creatures

And yet each unique and free

Like us

Each of us

There is no compare or judgment.

We all bring something special to this world.

We may be a bundle of past karma and DNA.

But yet we are but holy and pure.

Let us honor our purity

And break the bondage of envy and compare.

Connect to that golden thread

That weaves through all of us

And nature

And remember our song,

The song of eternal freedom.

I Believe I Can

History is full of people

Who came up with ideas unheard,

Unseen

As is mine.

It never stopped them

And it will not stop me.

People ridiculed;

They continued.

People laughed as they failed.

But they stood tall and carried on

Until they achieved,

And when they did, they laughed

And were celebrated

And so I too will continue.

I will carry on

And I will succeed,

For I believe I can,

For I know I can

And that is all that matters.

Tribe or No Tribe—I Am Happy

When you think you have found your tribe

And yet you have not

When you realize again

You are better alone

When you would try hard to fit in

And now you are unafraid to stand out

When you know there is a better way to do this

This thing called life

A way that is different to the masses

You find courage to follow your heart

To turn the other way

Even if it means to walk alone,

For suddenly you realize

You are happier alone

Than smothered by negativity.

You are more content in your world

Than inundated with others' regrets and baggage—

Or worse still, their fake promises, shallow interests,

and selfish motives.

When not all conversations serve you

And people you thought once important in your life,

You now cut chords with.

Someone once said

People come into your life for a reason,

season or to stay

And suddenly this rings true.

As you realize you have outgrown those you knew,

Where does one find their tribe?

Or does your tribe find you, adrift, call you to shore?

Perhaps until then you are happier alone.

I Am Unique One of a Kind

I need not be like anyone else;

I need not like what others like

Or do what others do

Or think their thoughts

Or accept their words.

I need not follow their choices

Or accept their ways to live as mine.

I am an individual,

Gifted with my own heart

My own soul

My own mind.

I can choose another way

Another route

Another thought

Another action,

One that is true to me.

It need not make sense to another;

This is not my concern,

For the only truth for me is to follow my own compass.

Their thoughts, their actions, their choices

Theirs, not mine

Are not my business.

My thoughts, my choices, my actions, my deeds

Are all my concern.

I need not copy the masses,

For I am a unique imprint of the divine—

One of a kind.

I can forge my own path in life,

Make my own choices, however bold.

Use different colors on my canvass,

Some bright, some gold

And a whole lot of love.

And this need not be another's;

I stand liberated,

Alone

And liberated,

Not bound by the choices dictated by society.

My values are different

And I stand strong whole in them.

For You, Mother

The wisdom in your eyes

The smile on your face

Lines of wisdom approach

But your inner child does not see that.

She still wants to play and laugh

Go to places, see new faces.

The crone in your being knows the wisdom of life—

The fruits of which are short

And yet in each moment, eternal.

Your stories light up your eyes

And sometimes find an inner knowing.

Sometimes a pain long forgotten,

Sometimes a laugh long wanting.

You are so beautiful, oh Mother

Just the way you are

And with each passing day,

Your beauty grows and knows no bounds.

Cherish the little girl inside you for she too is wise.

Laugh and live and live and laugh.

Treasure those hands that raised us.

Kiss those beautiful wrinkles

And smile

Your beautiful smile

Because when you do,

The night sky in your almond eyes

Lights up like a million stars

And sets a glow far and beyond

It touches the hearts of many,

Especially mine,

So never forget your smile.

The Power of Our Pack

We sense the unseen.

We prosper in our circles, in our packs.

It is time that we honor ourselves by honoring

the power of our circles,

For time immemorial our kind, the women kind,

the witch kind

Have roamed in packs, have immortalized the meaning

of community, of society, of friendship

Have soothed and calmed each other's wounds

With tears, with laughter, with lighthearted fun,

Have celebrated birth and death with equal austerity.

Our moon cycles unite us in a circle of life

that we have sadly been made to forget

And in our circle, we share our pain, our woes,

our cries, our ambitions, our laughter,

Our sensuality and our sexuality.

We come alive together as we balm each other's

wounds with our love, hugs and tears.

Us womenkind have a power in our unity.

Let us not forget our innate nature to be with,

support and love one another.

Let us remember our loyal and protective nature

of each other and cradle one another in grace,

In love and in light.

What is this new age feeling of animosity, jealousy,

envy and competition?

Why not lift each other up with our hearts instead

of pull each other or worse still clamber over

Each other to get to the top?

Why not believe that there is more than enough room

at the top,

Whatever and wherever this top might be?

And why not realize that if we pull each other up,

we are a stronger front?

Let us not divide in angst among ourselves only

to be the butt of many a chauvinist joke.

Let us grow in each other and let our branches tie

each of us together so that we may cast a

Web so strong that the mightiest of spider would take

pride in our work.

And let that web be the launch of any woman of any

kind of any type of any form to launch and

Take off to wherever she may wish, for the sky

is no limit for a woman supported by her kind.

Let us kindle and nurture our female friendships,

our treasures

And return to our true nature,

the nature of the wild wolf

Where she sniffs out danger for her tribe

And goes to the vast lengths of the sea to protect

her kind,

For she believes and holds true to her heart,

That a woman supported by a woman

is a force of nature that becomes unstoppable,

Unshakeable, unbreakable.

Oh my friends let us unite ever more now than ever

before and let us be one spirit in many bodies,

In unison we walk this earth and in grace,

we hold each other's hands and hearts

And allow us all, each and every one of us to prosper

today, tomorrow and for eternity.

Gaia

You may call her the Mother-Creator-God

of all beings and doings,

from the seas to the skies, from the ant to the tiger.

You may call her *Mother Nyx*[14],

for she has dominion over all things from the mud

and the dark.

You may call her the reverent *Durga*[15],

for she controls the skies and the winds

and the thoughts of humans from which

all perceived reality flows.

You may call her *Coatlicue*[16] as she gives birth

to the infant universe, like any infant, rascally and

Difficult to control.

Or you may call her *Hekate*[17], the old seer, the crone

And yet whatever name you call her by,

She remains.

She exists everywhere; for us to pause and see

A shelter of hope an abundance of love.

Mama Gaia endlessly gives and we endlessly take.

Her children, like brats, incessantly suck on her sweet

nectar where it almost runs dry her abundant breasts.

And yet like untrained monkeys,

the greed of her children knows no bounds.

They destroy her land and wreak havoc in her waters.

They kill the birds with their gases and pollute

the waters with their synthetics.

And what does Mama Gaia do?

She gives—

A love unheard of, unspoken and unseen,

One yet to be measured.

She endlessly provides in the hope and in the prayer

That her children will one day smile on her giving

That the love she gives through each leaf, in each tree,

in each root, in each branch,

In each wisp of wind will one day ground her

lost children.

By showing them grace, she believes they will hear

the sadness in the rhythm of her earth .

They will sense her sorrow and simply allow

her time to recover.

That is all she asks for—

Time to recover, to replenish her lost resources

so that her breasts can once again nourish.

Is that too much for a mother to ask from her child

for whom she unconditionally provides?

---

[14] *Nyx* in Greek mythology Nyx is the primordial goddess of the night. She is one of the earliest deities, born from Chaos, and is considered a powerful and ancient force. Nyx is often depicted as a dark and mysterious figure, and she gives birth to a variety of other significant deities and beings associated with the night and darkness.

[15] *Durga* is a powerful goddess in Hinduism, and she is often depicted as a warrior goddess and protective divine feminine force.

[16] *Coatlicue* is a major deity in Aztec mythology, and she is often considered a mother goddess associated with life, death, and fertility.

[17] *Hekate* is a goddess in ancient Greek religion and mythology. She is a complex deity associated with various aspects of life, magic, and the supernatural.

The Dance of My Psyche

I never learned the waltz, nor the salsa or the bachata

But my psyche is a flawless dancer,

Dancing to the tunes of society.

Today a false belief, tomorrow a questionable truth

Dancing to the beats of narrow beliefs

and close-minded ideas

Grooving to the tunes of lies, paradoxes and gossip

And when realizing the perils of such a dance of fire

Turning to a waltz with truth

With liberty, with thoughts as wide as open spaces

As deep as the black hole

As endless as the galaxies

Switching the tunes of mankind for the rhythm

of the trees and the hymn of the winds

The choir of the birds

The trumpet of the insects,

My psyche rejoices in this new dance.

It enjoys this new rhythm where it no longer must

keep up but rather can sway to the moment's music

And each moment, oh how full and rich it is.

And yet from time to time, my psyche wobbles

in its dance; it falls backwards to the past or

Anxiously looks ahead to the future,

and in the process without fail, always loses balance

Until my psyche awakes again from its relapse

and breathes once more the fresh air

And watches how a dead leaf rebirths a new leaf

How a crow protects its young.

My psyche smiles again

And dances in a way that it cares no more.

It finds its rhythm and sways

And moves and sways. Oh how natural this is

How beautiful and light it feels

How whole it is.

The One Who Knows

I meet her from time to time.

With every visit, I wish she would stay a little

while longer.

She is wise, she is me, but she stays in the shadows

although of pure light

A warm light.

Or is it I who keeps her in the shadows?

Why do I do that? I do love her company and I love

when she takes over,

For then I know I am my truth,

So why do I keep her in the shadows?

Am I afraid of her light,

By her relentless glow?

I know she knows;

She knows the depths of my soul, the sea of my talent.

Should I let her out forever?

What would happen?

Would I lose or gain everything?

Is there really anything that truly belongs to me for me

to lose in this world?

No.

So what do I have to lose if I let the One Who Knows

take over every sinew, vein, heartbeat in Me?

If I let her out of the shadows,

or maybe she doesn't need letting out,

Maybe I need to go into the shadows and be guided

by her light.

What will I find in the shadows?

Will I ever come out?

What if her light is but a fragment

of my vast imagination?

What if there is not enough light after all?

Why do I doubt?

Do I doubt my creation?

If I am created in the form of my creator,

surely the light from the One Who Knows

will protect Me?

Guide me, show me, help me face the shadows.

Do I need help in facing the shadows?

Why do I need help?

What is in the shadows?

Secrets and pain subdued, buried for eternity,

Pain that is mine and not mine

But yet I cannot live without going into the shadows.

And so I will go.

I will let the darkness engulf me,

penetrate my powers, overpower my senses

And I will breathe in the darkness.

I will not run.

I will not hide.

I will not ask for help.

I will look at the darkness;

the spells they carry I shall break.

The chains that lock me in I shall tear open.

Chest forward, eyes piercing, a glow in my heart

For I have no hate for the shadows but only love

Only love for everything that has been me

And sure enough, transcendence shows

That the One Who Knows was never a stranger

For she was sitting in the light

Waiting for me to arrive

For she is no separate to me or to the shadows.

For she and I have always been but one.

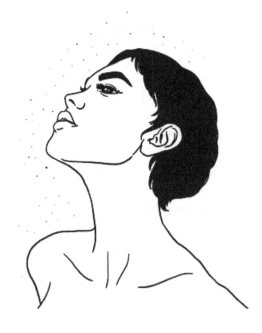

My Womb

Time immemorial us womenfolk have been told

that our womb

Our life force

Our seeds

Are to be harvested into babies.

No.

I say no.

I tell my womenfolk no.

In our womb,

Our precious ovaries

Resides an old wise woman.

She sits next to our seeds, our eggs

And waits,

Waits until it is time for an idea, a burning desire,

an art, a project to be born

To be birthed to.

Our womb, our life force is to birth,

Not only babies

But to our inborn, inner most, deepest talents,

our precious gifts that were embodied into our Seeds

and planted in the fire in the pit of our wombs.

Our job

Is to meditate them to light

To allow them to surface

To nurture them as we would a babe

To allow them to grow, to water them,

To allow them to flourish

And with them for us to flourish

To hymn and to dance, to write and to sing them into

prosperity, into love, into devotion

To allow our ovaries to do our dance and sing

our song—

The song of our souls.

Allow the song of our souls to surface

And let us sing all night long

Until the birds come out in shock at our voices

Our voices, singing at the top of the mountaintops

at the top of our lungs hurray, swaying our hips in a

toxic splendor, our eyes like bright moons shining

Unstoppable

Fierce like warriors of the night ready for battle

A battle of a different kind

A battle of our birth for our re-birth for our realization.

As we come down the mountaintops

And we greet our fellow men,

Respect them and carry on,

For we have a mission

And it is one for once not to rear children.

For this time,

It is to rear ourselves

Suppressed for so long

Deprived for so long

Forgotten for so long.

In our skirts

And our bare chests, we come hurling down, singing

the songs of our breasts, of our bellies—

Our bellies hot with desire to lung us out

To breathe us into oblivion,

to unite us in such a splendor

Of fireworks and of song,

No more deprivation.

We will never thirst or want for a love outside

Never a need for validation or appreciation no more

For we have found our truth

And it rests in the belly of all of us.

As we rub our bellies, caress the whirlpool

of talent within us,

We see a bright light up the sky as we are smiled upon,

for we have finally realized our truth

An energy that we never felt before.

Tears in our eyes roll freely; there is, alas,

nothing to hide.

There never was.

Our powerhouse is active; we are alive—

Abundant with talent—we flow, we live, we love

Our love so pure

So magnificent.

I birthed myself and so can you.

I can stand alone and so can you.

I evoked my seeds to germinate into the dreams

and talents of my soul

And so can you.

Manifest, manifest, manifest.

Sing your hymns, over your bones

As you resurrect.

Do not fail to do justice

To yourself

To your soul.

Rise and give birth to yourself

Before it is too late.

We owe it to the world

To our mothers and grandmothers

To their mothers and grandmothers

To the future and to the past

To you and to me.

Little Me, My Little Yoda

She laughs, she sings, she plays.

Little me is a bundle of joy,

light and a powerhouse of love.

As I close my eyes to embrace her,

She runs with the biggest smile and the brightest eyes

Happy to see me

Even as little as she is,

in her white dress with red flowers,

She is wise beyond years.

As I pick her up to embrace her,

She looks into my eyes and smiles—

An innocent smile, as if to say, There you are.

When I ask her if she has a message for me,

She simply smiles, takes her fingers and pulls up

my cheeks into a smile.

Like I said, she is a mini-Yoda wise beyond her years.

As she twirls and swirls and jumps up and down,

She knows no future, no past.

For her, the world is now

How did I get from that little girl to this woman?

I feel her energy and I realize my energy has not aged

a day.

I can still choose to see the world through her eyes—

To dance and to jump and to smile and to be happy

always every day in every way.

I feel her energy and I know

She wishes for me to follow my heart.

And so I ask my heart to show,

to guide where I need to go.

The answer will come

As it always does.

I never saw her as happy as I see her today.

She is happy that I am finally taking care of her.

She is happy to see me truly happy.

I give her one final embrace and let her into my soul

As we both became one, for we were never two

As we both manifest into the light.

Even now she is inside.

She has always been inside of me.

My soul is one

And always has been one,

There is no little soul and big soul.

It is only my body that knows time and age.

The little girl and the grown woman are all the same—

No separation, no difference, complete union.

Not Withered, but Wizened

Strings of white light now catch my once ebony hair.

In the eyes of the world, I am graying.

In the eyes of the soul, I am brightening.

Yet I walk the streets covering the silver wisps

that threaten to escape my scarf, my band, my cap.

I should have colored them today

And yet here I am attempting and hoping

to camouflage them.

I stare at myself in the mirror—

The youth of younger days fast fading,

a skin once taut now creasing

Like a wrinkled cloth that will not iron out

But yet I try to pull the lines apart,

Temporarily rejoicing at the glimmer of a taut past

Until the skin stubbornly crumples back,

arrogant of my pursuit.

I crumble inside.

I am aging.

I am no longer a young swan but now an old hag.

I am no longer a bombshell but now a hollow face.

But all this happens on the outside.

On the inside,

Rests a different story,

I have no age and so no fear.

I feel wise beyond my years.

I awake in the morning with an inexplainable joy.

I no longer need to worry about another,

For I know who I am.

True, I am no longer a maiden on the outside

But the peace of the crone in the inside is far superior

to any youth I once may have had.

And who is to say that time has become past?

For is it not all an illusion that is not meant to last

And I surpass and rise above

And I look down below and see a body

that never was mine

A temporary abode while on this plane

And I smile

For there is no age where I come from.

There is no body where I reside

An eternal light am I

A power so strong.

I have lived my time on this earth,

with many a splendid a victory, many a letdown

And yet here I am in my glory with the silver wisps

and the wrinkles galore

And I know that youth is fickle

And the wisdom I have now is pure treacle,

Which I savor with each breath.

Now I guide the young maidens and my sinews rejoice

for having past that age.

No longer a fear, no longer a doubt

Clarity and confidence are the name of my game

As I walk on, proud with my silver mane.

Grateful to... Me

I never thanked myself until this day

And what a cathartic release it was

As I looked at myself

And saw an incredible woman stare back.

Such a beautiful smile

Such confidence

Such valor

Such a stride

Such power in her voice

Why did not I ever see all this before?

Why did not I ever thank her for all that she is

and who she is?

For all those times I cast her aside?

For the time she bravely and barely 7 stood up against

her dad three times her size to protect her mum

Or for her kindness when she pushed to celebrate her

sister's birthday when Mum and Dad were fighting

Or her bravery when she confronted her Dad to allow

her sister to be on the radio

Or when she decided to study law in a foreign country

Even when she had never slept outside her home alone

Or when she walked alone at night on the street

for the first time

Or when she volunteered at a law clinic

and at a charity shop

Or when she nursed a friend's broken heart

And the time that she decided to become

her own woman.

When she decided it was time to travel on her own,

Quit her job and swim with manta rays alone

To climb a mountain

Go silent for a week!

Join a monastery and shave her head!

What a joy it is to see her journey;

What a joy it is to see her grow.

How could I ever say mean things to her,

A heart so pure?

And so I vow on this day to always love myself true

To thank every cell, every vibration in my body

To thank my being each day

And to hug myself tight before I sleep each night.

I Love All of Me

I spent a night by myself in all my glory,

Touching and caressing myself like no lover had,

Loving myself in beauty and in simplicity.

Why is nakedness frowned upon?

The simple human body holds so much,

The female body a map of unlocked desires.

I spent a night with myself,

Loving and appreciating myself.

It was a night of pure and tender love

As I embraced all of me—

The parts that I see as perfect

The parts that I ridicule and want to change,

For I realized in that night,

There is nothing of this body that I reside in that I would change.

All of it perfectly created in my Creator's grace and in my Creator's form,

For I am perfect even though the world defines perfect

as never good enough

I spent a night with myself in ecstasy

And I realized that I love all of me.

Who Am I Now?

Where was I before here?

Do you know?

Who was I before here?

Do I know?

Who am I now?

I do not know—

An intensity and lightness

A paradox of sorts

A burning inside

A cry out of my womb

Who am I?

I demand to know.

You know already.

The same riddle answer I receive

A thousand faces I have had

Another thousand personalities—

I can choose to be anyone.

Who do I choose to be?

Do I choose to be any?

My past selves all dead

My future selves to be decided by me

What about now?

Who do I choose to be now?

Who am I now?

My Guru

I am the roots, the trees, the branches, the leaves

The ant, the frog, the bird that sings

The fish that swims

The woman that sways

A blade of grass, the mighty man

The star, the dust, the sun, the moon

The galaxies—

All of it I am.

What pride can I have in me for nothing belongs

to me;

I do not belong to me.

I can only heal if I submit my vessel to the Creator

of All that is.

So what pride can I have when no morsel

of me is mine?

None of it belongs to me in birth nor in death.

It never was mine.

A vessel of god, an instrument to be played

To the Creator's melody

Seek your inner guru.

Find your inner extraordinaire

Because you are God.

God is in me, in us.

And if that is so, how dare I rely on another's wisdom

to navigate my life?

No one else can see, do, or be me

Or walk my life's path.

It is mine only to follow

To cultivate

To root.

No one can support me or transcend for me.

Both are my tasks to do.

No Jesus, no Mohammed, no Buddha sought help.

The only help they had was that from the Creator.

So truly the only relationship that matters

Is the one I have with the Creator.

I am but another vessel here to do the Creator's

bidding.

I must forego.

I do forego

And let go of all

Everything that was ever taught to me

About God

About Life

About Death

About Birth

About Love

About Loss

About Pride

All of it a lie

All of it false

For inside I must go

To seek my guru

The one who knows it all

The one who knows the truth I seek

The liberty I crave from these chains

The one who knows the past, the future

The one who knows what I must do

Why I am on this plane of existence

Whatever I am here to do.

And so today I succumb

To ask no more or doubt no more the Creator's power,

the magic.

I promise to heal all those who need the Creator's

healing,

For I know I carry the divinity in me.

The cosmic womb

Wants to burst forth

To love unconditionally

For me to do what is intended.

All the buddhas

All the saints

All the magic there exists is all there.

The black hole is open.

The light shines

And I must walk this path

With or without anyone

Whether or not anyone believes

Whether or not anyone understands.

If I must stand alone in this journey, so be it,

For this is my path

The path to create, to love, to be, to heal

The path to everlasting divinity.

To the Creator I pray and my one and only true love

That ever will be.

The Creator writes this.

The Creators speaks this.

Lights flashing, defenses melting, egos dying

I lose it all for that one true love.

The one true glimpse of divinity

I lose it all.

I surrender it all

For that warmth, the eternal light.

I give it all so that I may do my Creator's bidding,

For it is to my Creator that I return.

And I pray to the Creator to guide me,

For I am nothing but putty in my Creator's hands.

None of this belongs to me,

Not my fingers

Not these words

Not my life

Not my voice

And yet here I am to do the Creator's bidding

With a touch of free will in me,

But I choose to use my free will to follow my heart

and soul

To live my truth finally.

No more confusion

No more resistance

No more falsities

The body may give in;

The mind will open.

And I will continue,

For I am the blade of grass

The universe eternal

The galaxies divine

A body of infinite wisdom

A heart of infinite talent

An inheritance of inner power

Capacities beyond measure

All these await

Await for me to break from the clasps of all

that no longer serves me.

It is time to fire the servants called Doubt and Anxiety

So that I may return to my Source,

Return to Love,

For it is there that I must reside.

In silence, contentment and fortitude, I stay,

Until I am summoned to do my Creator's bidding.

Turn Your Achilles Heel to Gold... and Let Go

Through the sands of time

And through the ages

Who have stood are those

Who have had the courage to turn their Achilles heel

to gold

To churn their wounds into wombs

To birth their truth,

For is there anything that can shine as bright

as your soul?

Once you're allowed to lead yourself through life,

It is only then that you become unstoppable

A force of nature to be reckoned with,

Breaking from what you have been told

Recognizing the lion that you always were

even if reared with sheep

Forsaking all religions and relations

Stepping into the unknown

With no direction.

And while to many on the outside you may be lost,

A deep kindling inside whispers if you pay attention:

"It is only now that you are found."

The soul moves at its own pace;

It knows not time nor hurry.

But so conditioned I am to running

It is challenging to learn to walk.

And so I eagerly look for signs,

Even though I know

All I need to do is let go.

Healing Tree

I basked in your embrace, oh great one.

You held me and comforted me.

I felt no lack for a loved one.

You held my hand and allowed me to heal.

You gave your energy to heal me.

You allowed me to rest under your shade in the palm

of your leaves.

You allowed me to breathe a while, to just be.

And when I awoke, I was revived.

Grateful to your bark,

Thankful for your energy, oh loving tree.

It Is I Who Chose This Test

Many a light years have I travelled

Many a grave I have laid to rest

And yet death is unbaffled

And continues to test.

My soul, a fire burning bright,

Inflicts many a lesson

A contract made on another plane

The terms of which remain

So here I am on Mother Earth

Subject to conditions, with no regret.

A deeper knowing gradually seeps in

Like a snake slowly unfurling.

As the recognition of this connection grows,

Many questions drown

And yet many a seed is sowed

For what and who can I question

When it is I who chose this test?

The cycle of cause and effect.

The Gateway to the Universe

I have never seen such beautiful eyes

The entire universe in them

The feeling of being surreal and real all at once.

Looking into those dark eyes with stars in them,

I am the universe and the universe is me.

The past wilted away like a flower to give root to the

truth that I am today

The strength that I carry.

Dead leaves of the past bring fruit the leaves of today

The beauty of today.

My childhood gone, no longer real

The future unknown and just as unreal.

The universe eternal

Me, eternal

A truth long forgotten in the currents of time

Being brought forth by those dark starry eyes

Passage of time eternal or maybe not

Pain, tears, fear real but maybe not?

A oneness

An eternal truth springing forth like a flower

A circle complete

Old wounds laid to rest.

Her dark starry eyes know it all.

She was me as I was once her.

She knows and reminds me that I know too.

What more will it take to remember

The truth?

Is it not enough that the sun kisses the morning

each day

And the moon caresses the night with her grace?

Is it not enough that even through cement,

a plant can take root

Or that a bird defies the law of gravity

Or the reality that I have created each and every single

second and moment good or bad in this life

Or the ultimate truth that I chose this life

and that it did not choose me.

Her starry eyes show me the way to eternity

To the galaxies, the lubnae and beyond

To the black holes

The unseen planets

Worlds unknown and yet known.

Who am I if not the universe?

As truth would have it,

I hold the five elements within me

The same elements that make up the world:

Fire, air, earth, water and of course, ether

All of it in me

All of it outside of me.

So is it not true that

I am the universe

And the universe is me?

Act Like a Lady... No More

I was always taught to behave

To sit like a lady, to act like a lady

To smile like a lady, to speak like a lady

To be a lady

Until I grew up and questioned,

What is this niceness that I was taught?

Enough sugar to kill a person from diabetes.

I realized that my inner wild nature had been curtailed

and modified to a "lady" that was never meant to be.

I realized that I had within me the power

of the maiden, the mother and the crone

And that the wild woman in me was screaming

to be born.

In a society that has often consumed many a witch

when even though the word "wit" means Wise,

A wild woman is seen by many to break all rules

and throw things around.

But is that true?

Embracing and honoring my wild nature means

living for myself.

It means embracing my wants and desires and seeing

to the ends where they take me.

It means breaking society's norms and finding out

my own rules and norms and paths.

It means following my voice of intuition rather than

the million voices outside of me that I had given

authority to live my life!

It means to honor myself in every way

Whatever way and route that might be and look like.

Whether it be ugly, or confrontational,

It means embracing the ugliness and looking at it
with tenderness.

It means honoring and coming into my strength
and finding the strength in my voice to speak

To speak up

To air my rage every time that I am wronged

To take pride in my work

To take pride in my step in my bounce,
in my hips, in my breasts

To own my body

To own myself

To own my demons and embrace them

To resolutely allow my voice to be heard.

Do I have to be loud to do this?

No.

Do I have to shout and scream to be heard?

Definitely not, but if need be,

I hesitate not.

I allow myself to be me.

The me that was suppressed

and denied so long ago

Has been let out

To speak for herself

To fight for herself

To find herself

To honor all those witches and wild women

that came before her and those that will come

After her

To bless her

To be guided by her

For the time for silence is dead

The time for liberation is alive

The time to be heard is now

For if not now

Then when?

And if not me, then who?

I Grow Silent

A heaviness descends like a fog,

A mysticism I have not experienced before

From words to silence

From silence to a deep stillness.

I do not wish to speak no more

I naturally wish to stay silent.

But will this world let me?

Perhaps it is not so much about silence

But more about observing

And awareness.

I feel solemn.

I feel numb.

I do not understand this and yet I do.

What does it mean to have balance

between your two minds?

How does a spiritual coexist

with the rational mind?

How are the two intertwined or aligned?

And yet I have seen many a saint do the same.

They do not fall short of their worldly duties

in the face of their spiritual pursuits

For the way of the spiritual is the world

And so the saints, our predecessors,

the truth seekers that came before us

Insist on the observance of worldly duties

Even after a period of inner retreat.

They insist on a return to the world

To serve the rest of mankind.

But then, what is this I am feeling?

Is it a feeling or yet another dream?

Am I moving closer to my Source?

Is it my nature to withdraw?

Is this what I am being called to do right here,

right now?

A heavy feeling descends

An energy, a force

Or am I seeing the mirage of this world

for the first time?

I have little interest in the materiality.

Displaced is what I feel.

A natural silence descends upon me

Where mid-sentence I lose words to say

An oddity or my reality

I am unsure and yet these words I write spill

from somewhere.

So is it really silence that is to be observed

Or is it truth?

A message in meditation

I am still not living my truth.

What is my truth?

Is that not the journey that I am on?

Why do I feel so lost and yet found?

Why do I feel like silence is where it all lies

Where it all falls into place?

Suddenly, I have some answers,

But even more questions than ever before arise.

A mysticism unknown

My words taken

I am silent.

What Is My Truth?

Something is happening.

Something needs to come out and be released.

Or is it that something needs to be realized?

My natural state

All the saints before me

And all those who will come after me

No different are they from me in being.

Two arms, two legs, a torso, a head

A skeletal system, a nervous system

Flesh and bones

So

If we are but the same,

What prevents me from harnessing my gifts?

From realizing my unlimited potential

From living out my destiny

What prevents me from becoming self-actualized?

What prevents me from filling my cup with eternal

love, a faithful love, an everlasting glory?

What prevents me from seeing things as they are?

Is it me who prevents me?

Is it the world?

For if I am the maker of my world

And if I choose to see and to live in truth,

Then nothing should prevent me.

Are the lids on my eyes heavier than I thought

them to be?

Has the fog thickened over the time that my spirit

has been on earth?

Is there a lot that still remains to be turned

and churned?

For the heavy lids and the thick fog to be lifted

and cleared

But yet I know I have made headway

Yet I know I am and I will get there.

I asked someone, a stranger almost

If she was living her truth

If one points one finger out,

One must not forget that four point back.

And so the question to me remains:

Am I living my truth?

But what is my truth?

A Moving Meditation

There is so much distraction in this world.

How do we listen

With so much noise

But the noise is outside

In the inside a serene silence.

A silent Om echoes throughout

With each breath a birth and a death.

Why go out and let the outside noise bother me?

Why not tune in

All the time

Always in every moment?

How beautiful it is to tune in

Surrounded by noise.

The noise no longer touches me.

Surrounded by others' energy, it no longer bothers me.

How beautiful it is to rest inside

In the arms of my beloved

In the embrace of true love

How quiet it is

How incredibly peaceful.

I rest my head on the hum of my heartbeat.

I let the energy bounce off me and not seep in.

My shoulders relax as I tune in to my breath.

This is the meaning of meditation

The moment I tune in.

A smile spreads across my lips

In peace with all that this moment brings

A grounding I feel in my feet

As I breathe into my soul.

Always connected

And I can always reach within.

I am never too far from peace.

How can I be?

For peace is me

And I am a moving meditation.

The Embodiment of the Divine Feminine

I am the divine feminine embodied in this body.

I am the one I seek, for I know

I know that I know and she knows

My soul knows.

I am the one I have been seeking

Legs wide, open arms calling to sky,

Giving birth to a splendor

Inside of me.

I am the divine feminine that I seek

That I have long thirsted for.

I am she and she is me;

She has always been inside.

And now she is starting a fire in my belly

And announcing her entry.

It is time.

Oh, it has been a while.

Oh, it has taken time.

For my eyes to see

For my heart to beat

For no one

But me

For my hairs to rise

To no other sound than my own voice.

Oh, it is time

For her to take over me.

I Embrace All of You

I embrace you—

All of you

Your vulnerabilities

Your perceived insecurities

Your karmic pains

Your abundance

Your laughter

Your sexuality

Your bliss.

I embrace all of you.

In me, you will find nothing but love

Only love.

I embrace all of you.

Is it not time that you came to me?

Oh dear soul of mine,

Quieten no more.

Guide me so that as one, we can do our work—

What we are here to do.

I embrace all of you.

Will you embrace all of me?

Are you not already in me?

What Is the Love That I Seek— Can It Be Outside?

To feel the flow of words flow through you like music

Like stardust

With the ease of butter on hot toast

Or the silence of a raindrop resting on a lotus petal

As natural as the vivid blue in the sky

Or the skip of a heartbeat as eyes meet

Or the song of a bird in the morning

And the cooing in the evening

Or when nature holds you awestruck

As it unabashedly parades its beauty

Or as colorful fish wander in the depths

Oblivious to their beauty

As flawless as the breath I breathe,

What is this life than all these combined?

What is the love that I seek and can it be outside?

For is it not already here in every sight, sound,

and breath inside?

Jump

Don't think; just jump!

The voice yelled.

True courage, that plans sometimes devour

I never thought of myself as courageous.

I never thought of myself as brave.

I simply did what the fire in my stomach

What the beat in my heart

What the drum in my throat echoed me to do.

I stood at the edge of the cliff,

Smiling at the faces in the water laughing

Tempted to join.

I got ready to jump.

I stood at the edge of the rock

And heard a voice inside commanding loud and clear,

Jump.

Arms wide open and welcoming

Head to the sky.

I took a chance and jumped.

Turned my back on everything I knew.

I dived into a canyon without a guide or map.

My instinct, my only navigation

Alive and telling me to let go and go on.

Liberated, heart beating ferociously and with a smile

brewing from inside.

One breath at a time I walked on,

Trusting the arms of the universe

wrapped around me.

On each bike ride and each interaction with a stranger

With each jump to catch the fish

With each boat ride

With each handshake with each smile with each laugh

A human bond, a human connection

All through,

Perhaps there is truth in what they say:

Happiness attracts happiness.

Love attracts love and so it is,

Each person crossing my path

carrying a message

for me

I know this to be true.

I know this in my core.

And so without looking back,

I jumped.

Wounded Gifted Soldiers

Wounded soldiers, we walk on,

Each carrying a deep wound and an even deeper gift.

In solitude, we cry out.

Outside, we soldier on

Sadness our great master

Aloneness the wise crone

Wounded and yet not

Gifted and yet ignorant

Deeply seeded, cocooned like a butterfly in a pupa

Waiting, watching, wanting

To release, to break free

To embrace our wounds as our vulnerable wings

Soft yet strong

For in our wounds seat our gifts and our gifts

hold our freedom to be.

What are my gifts? I beseech.

When will it be revealed to me?

Or do I already know and cannot see?

If so, what clouds my vision?

Where are my wings?

Or are they here and I do not feel?

I March On

War I fight each day.

Do I blame them or do I look within?

What is it that I fight and why?

Is there an end in sight?

Victory perhaps?

Or defeat?

What is this war and why do I engage?

Energy so precious that I cultivate

Without a thought,

I waste in battles that have long fallen

And yet the wounds remain ripe as yesterday.

And I engage,

Realizing this no longer serves me.

How do I now willfully abstain?

These battles prove endless

And spiral me to devastation.

I cut all chords

And refuse to engage.

Call me weak or a coward.

I resign from your words,

Your opinions mere sounds

That no longer resonate.

I turn away from this battle ground

Alone and in despair at time lost,

Only to realize that my soul knows no time or space.

It knows only its evolution.

And so I lift my head to the sky with a fresh resolve

A vow to myself

To honor my original agreement

Whatever that might be, to ignore the mechanics

of the world and the functions of society

To go as my heart desires

To live a true glory

For I do not know how many days remain to my name,

But I do know wasting another breath on a war

or a battle is not my game.

And so I march on with a new resolve

To self-knowledge I tally on

Unafraid of the lonely days ahead

Bold-breasted I march on.

Wounds I do carry

Unfinished business to resolve

But with a new purpose to create the life

of the destiny of my soul,

I march on.

A Song for My Soul

A wise little girl I once knew,

Stars in her eyes,

A heart full of dreams.

She lost her smile one day,

Traded her toys for tears, anger and grief

Not knowing what she lost.

She carried on,

Accepting tears as dolls

Until once upon a day

A wise old lady that she knew so well

Came to her and said,

"Sweet child of divine a light of mine,

You have forgot your source.

You have forgot your treasure.

Here I gift you a basket of pain

And a smile.

Wear the smile as you carry this basket of pain

And when you find your light,

let go the basket in the river of Karma.

Let it float away.

Attach not yourself to the basket,

For it was never yours to carry.

Hand it over to the rightful

And bid your work adieu.

Your work, sweet child of divine,

Is neither to cry nor to sorrow.

Oh sweet child of divine,

Yours is a work of love.

Why do you look at me questioningly?

Touch your heart and tell me I lie.

You know I speak the truth

Because I am you and you me

So, sweet child of divine,

Promise me a promise—

A sacred promise between you and me.

Let us not forget our divinity.

Let us smile and laugh and play and dance and sing

as much as we can while our heart beats

And our breath sings.

And until the last song

To which our ears finally close,

Let us smile."

ABOUT THE AUTHOR

SADAFF HABIB, born in Kenya and of Indian heritage, currently calls Dubai, UAE, her home. She is a New York qualified lawyer and works as an independent arbitrator. Beyond her legal pursuits, Sadaff is a poet and inspirational speaker, utilizing her creative voice to connect with others.

Navigating through the rich tapestry of her multicultural background, Sadaff weaves words that transcend borders and resonate with the human experience. Her poetry serves as a reflection of personal journeys, capturing the essence of wounds, resilience, love, healing and the intricate dance between light and shadow.

In addition to her legal career, Sadaff passionately embraces her role as an inspirational speaker, with a mission to compassionately guide individuals toward their own inner light. Her words, both on paper and on stage, aspire to uplift, inspire, and foster connections that transcends cultural boundaries. She also works on a personal basis with individuals to guide them to their healing and authentic selves.

For a deeper exploration of Sadaff's compassionate guidance and poetic expressions, connect with her online at:

www.sadaffhabib.com